One Small Boat

ALSO BY KATHY HARRISON

Another Place at the Table

One Small Boat

The Story of a Little Girl,
Lost Then Found

Kathy Harrison

JEREMY P. TARCHER/PENGUIN
a member of Penguin Group (USA) Inc.
New York

JEREMY P. TARCHER/PENGUIN
Published by the Penguin Group
Penguin Group (USA) Inc., 375 Hudson Street, New York, New York 10014, USA • Penguin
Group (Canada), 90 Eglinton Avenue East, Suite 700, Toronto, Ontario, M4P 2Y3, Canada
(a division of Pearson Penguin Canada Inc.) • Penguin Books Ltd, 80 Strand, London
WC2R 0RL, England • Penguin Ireland, 25 St Stephen's Green, Dublin 2, Ireland (a division of
Penguin Books Ltd) • Penguin Group (Australia), 250 Camberwell Road, Camberwell, Victoria
3124, Australia (a division of Pearson Australia Group Pty Ltd) • Penguin Books India Pvt Ltd,
11 Community Centre, Panchsheel Park, New Delhi–110 017, India • Penguin Group (NZ),
Cnr Airborne and Rosedale Roads, Albany, Auckland 1310, New Zealand (a division of
Pearson New Zealand Ltd) • Penguin Books (South Africa) (Pty) Ltd, 24 Sturdee Avenue,
Rosebank, Johannesburg 2196, South Africa

Penguin Books Ltd, Registered Offices:
80 Strand, London WC2R 0RL, England

Most Tarcher/Penguin books are available at special quantity discounts for bulk
purchase for sales promotions, premiums, fund-raising, and educational needs.
Special books or book excerpts also can be created to fit specific needs.
For details, write Penguin Group (USA) Inc. Special Markets,
375 Hudson Street, New York, NY 10014.

Library of Congress Cataloging-in-Publication Data

Harrison, Kathy.
One small boat: the story of a little girl, lost then found / Kathy Harrison.
p.   cm.
ISBN 1-58542-465-X
1. Foster children—Massachusetts—Biography.   2. Foster home care—Massachusetts—Case
studies.   3. Foster mothers—Massachusetts—Biography.   4. Harrison, Kathy.
I. Title.
HV883.M4H38   2006   2005054886
362.73'3092—dc22
[B]

Printed in the United States of America
1   3   5   7   9   10   8   6   4   2

BOOK DESIGN BY AMANDA DEWEY

Author's Note

This is a work of nonfiction. I have rendered the events recounted in this book to the best of my recollection. Some names and identifying characteristics have been altered to protect the privacy and anonymity of individuals, especially children, involved. In a few cases, individuals described may be composites of several people involved in an event.

To

Noni and Susan,
models of inspiration

Acknowledgments

My husband, Bruce, deserves most of the credit for this book. Writing a book with seven children under the age of ten in the house was only possible because of the husband and father he is. My children, Bruce Jr., Nathan, Amanda, Ben, Neddy, Angie, Karen, and Phoebe, have been unfailingly supportive, not just with my writing but also with the bevy of little ones who are the recipients of unconditional kindness and acceptance.

My editor at Tarcher, Sara Carder, let me find and use my own voice. My agent at Curtis Brown, Maureen Walters, has believed in me from the beginning.

Ted Oakley, Alice Oakley, Carl Warden, and Vickie Warden

of Foster Angels of West Texas have made my life so much easier with their generosity. I thank you every day.

Finally, I want to acknowledge the wise and caring men and women who have led me in my quest to help repair broken childhoods. I so often turn to the words of Meredith Wiley, Martha Beck, Mary Pipher, Dr. Phil, Robin Karr-Morse, T. Berry Brazelton, Torey Hayden, Marian Wright Edelman, and Maya Angelou for guidance and inspiration.

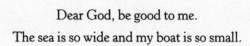

Dear God, be good to me.
The sea is so wide and my boat is so small.

One Small Boat

Prologue

In May of 2003, right after the release of my first book, *Another Place at the Table,* and just before I jumped back into foster parenting with both feet, I received a small packet from my social worker, Susan Crane. I had asked her some months earlier if it was possible for me to have a list of all the children I had cared for over the past fifteen years, and thanks to the marvels of the computer age, she was able to comply. The list was complete and a little scary. There were more than one hundred twenty names on it.

For the next several hours, I pored over that list. As I read the names, the faces and stories of each child came back to me. There was eight-month-old Elijah, whose wrists were still raw from the rope he had been tied up with. And eleven-year-old Katara. She spent a week with us, recuperating from the surgery she needed to repair the injuries she sustained when her step-brother raped her. I will never forget Juanita. She cried when a judge ordered her returned to her alcoholic mother. "It's not fair," she sobbed on her last day with us. "You let me stay with you until I love you, and then I have to leave." She was right, of course. There is little that is fair about foster care.

I can rattle off the bare statistics. Every day more than seven hundred children come into foster care in this country because of suspected abuse or neglect. One-third of those children will never go home to their original families again. One-third who do go home will be back in care again before they reach adulthood. There are more than 550,000 children in the child welfare system in this country. The number is astounding, so large that most people can't comprehend it. Its enormity excuses our tendency to forget that these are not numbers but real little people.

I write for many reasons. I write out of my personal need to examine my world and explore my own motives. I write as catharsis so that the horror my children live will not eat me up and leave me bitter and cynical. I write to provide a counterbalance to the reality that a child is more than five times as likely to be killed while in foster care than while at home and that children in care are abused three times as often. But I write for another reason. I want people to see the real children hiding within the statistics. It is easier to ignore the 550,000 than it is to ignore Ashley, a four-year-old who had been videotaped having sex with her brother.

Prologue

This book is about a lot of children. It tells the stories of Jazzy and Crystal, Priscilla and Maggie. It is also a story about my daughter, Karen, who has had to fashion a childhood around the comings and goings of a band of temporary siblings. Mostly though, this book is about Daisy, the child I almost didn't take. She was crazy was what I was told. She needs more than a family will be able to offer. Like all children, Daisy was a teacher. She taught me about strength and courage and resiliency and finding joy in the ordinary. I also learned about loving and losing and that happy endings are often what we make for ourselves.

One

So, what do you think?"

"It's perfect. Just what I had in mind."

My husband, Bruce, and I stood in the doorway of what we referred to as "the littles'" room. Until recently, the space had been a gloomy and cramped bedroom, so shabby as to be nearly uninhabitable. Now, after weeks of plaster dust and splinters, Bruce had transformed it into a spacious, airy retreat. The original walls had been ripped out to pick up extra footage from the attic. Bruce had installed Sheetrock, painted it a soft gray, and laid new carpeting over the floor. Four small iron beds hugged the walls under snug, low eaves. Each bed was covered with a brightly colored quilt. A large wooden dollhouse sat in one corner, its occupants waiting patiently at a minuscule kitchen table. There was a box of dress-ups under one window, and a trunk filled with dolls and doll clothes under the second. A small round table and four child-sized chairs sat in the middle of the floor. It was a dream of a room, all the more appreciated because we were a family rather desperately in need of space.

Bruce and I were foster parents. At this time, four of our six biological and adopted children were still living at home and we were usually temporary parents to three or four other children in need of shelter at any given time. We had decided the previous year that we would provide care only to girls. Doing so made everything from arranging bedroom space to buying clothes and toys easier. We made an exception on occasion, especially in order to keep a brother and sister together, but for the most part we stuck to this decision and found it worked well for all of us.

Although our house was large, we were still bursting at the seams, especially on a busy weekend when we often provided emergency care for an extra child or two. Every inch of space was littered with the accoutrements of busy children: musical instruments, skis, tennis rackets, and balls of every conceivable size and weight. Life had not always been like this for us. When we started house hunting eight years earlier, we had a very manageable three children. We were looking for something small and easy to maintain. What we found was this barn of a house with ancient plumbing and no insulation.

It was typical of many rural New England farmhouses built in the middle of the last century. Like families in those less complicated times, it was built to last. With six bedrooms, it seemed built for children as well. Aside from a flourish of Victorian ginger-bread trim, it was unpretentious. The wide plank floors had withstood one hundred fifty years of muddy boots and spilled milk. Odd closets were perfect for games of hide and seek, and the long curved banister invited sliding.

In spite of its many problems, we bought the house, enam-ored not just of the oversized windows and nine-foot ceilings but of the community as well. Driving down Main Street is like stepping into a Norman Rockwell painting. Small children head toward the river for an afternoon of fishing, and long-married couples wave from front porches. It is an unusual Sunday after-noon breeze that doesn't carry the sounds of a softball game from the park down the street.

Maybe it was fate, or perhaps nature really does abhor a vac-uum, but the extra bedrooms cried out to be filled. When a child from my preschool program needed a home, Bruce and I were happy to oblige. I had always wanted a girl, and Angie felt like my daughter from the day she arrived. Her older sister, Neddy, soon joined us as well. We got a Massachusetts license to pro-vide foster care in preparation for our daughters' impending adoption. It seemed foolish to us, since we didn't intend to take more children, but it was a necessary first step in what proved to be a three-year process.

What we hadn't anticipated was the crushing need for foster parents in our area. In spite of the peace in our hill-town commu-nity, we were no more immune to the problems that plague families than any larger town. Poverty, drug abuse, and inadequate housing set the stage for neglect and abuse here as it does elsewhere. Only a few years earlier, a two-year-old child was beaten nearly to death by her father just a mile from my back door. Our social service agency covered the largest geographic area in the state. Every day the call would go out for social workers to find beds for children, and there were never enough beds. Since social services now had our number, they called us often. The stories I heard from the workers were drawn from the newspaper headlines. How could we say no to a child who had been beaten by his mother? Who can turn down a baby found on a doorstep? Not me and not Bruce as it turns out. Child followed child. We bought a van and began buying groceries in bulk. Still, it was many months before I could identify myself as a foster parent without cringing.

The stories of foster parents abusing their small charges made the evening news often enough to leave the impression that most foster parents were in it for the money, caring little about children. Unfortunately, there are some pretty grim homes out there. After a few months of fielding calls from desperate social workers, it was clear why. The math was simple. There were not then, and are not now, enough families willing to tolerate the disruption of abused children moving in and out of their lives. I know there are people who use the seventeen dollars a day they receive as a stipend for the care of a child to stretch a meager paycheck. I know there are people who find easy victims among children who have known no other role. Thankfully, those homes are rare, but they are the ones people hear about. In those first months I acknowledged being a foster mother with the same enthusiasm I would have mustered for admitting I did cosmetic research on pet bunnies.

While Bruce worked on the room, our three current foster children camped out in the den. Clothes, toys, and books were in boxes and piles all over the house. Everything felt chaotic and cluttered, and we were all a bit out of sorts from the disruption. I couldn't wait to move the girls' things into their new digs and get our lives back to what passed for normal in our family.

"How long do you suppose it will be before home-finding wants to fill up that empty bed?" Bruce asked as we looked over his handiwork.

"Not long. I turned down three girls in the past two weeks." We were approaching the holidays, a time when too much stress, too much alcohol, and not enough money took its toll on families. As a result, we all became busier. "I was thinking about asking for a baby. How would you feel about that?"

Bruce gave me a sideways glance that was far from encouraging. "I thought we were going to take a break from babies for a while. We all tend to get a bit too attached, and we're getting a little old to consider adopting again."

"Hey! Speak for yourself," I answered with a laugh. "Let's call the girls. They can't wait to start moving their clothes in." We had three girls living with us at the time, and for a change, nobody was in crisis. All three had problems, of course. The kinds of loss and trauma that land a child in foster care seldom hit a kid without leaving some emotional scars, but this group seemed remarkably stable, especially compared to some other children I had cared for in recent years.

Crystal was a beautiful eight-year-old girl. Honey-colored curls fell well past her shoulders. Her features were even and delicate, and she had slight dimples in each cheek. Even her teeth were perfect, straight and white, without the too-large look that most second teeth have for a few years.

Crystal's mother, Patty, had been only fourteen when she gave birth to Crystal. For five years she and her daughter lived with Patty's aunt. It was a good arrangement. Patty got some much-needed support and guidance from her aunt, and Crystal had the advantage of a loving, experienced surrogate mother for those important first years. But shortly before Crystal started school, the arrangement fell apart. There were power struggles between mother and great-aunt over Crystal's care and disagreements over Patty's increasingly active social life. After one particularly heated altercation, Patty packed her things and moved to a tiny apartment with the five-year-old child, who was more like a little sister than a daughter to her nineteen-year-old mother.

From the first, raising a child alone was a struggle for Patty. She still wanted to party, as she had in the past, but now there was no built-in babysitter. More and more often as the months went by, Crystal was left to fend for herself while Patty went out. Crystal seldom got to school on time, and when she did show up, she was tired and hungry. But it takes a lot more than poor attendance and no breakfast to cause a school to call in social services. Life managed to limp by for Crystal, as it does for so many children who live on the fringes. It might have continued that way had her apartment building not caught on fire one night. The fire department came and discovered the then seven-year-old alone at midnight. Crystal waited in a hotline home for two days before her mother called the police to find out where her child was.

Ideally, Crystal should have been placed with the aunt who had raised her, but the aunt had a new boyfriend with a criminal record, and social services wouldn't allow Crystal to stay in a house where he was living. By default, Crystal ended up with us.

When she had first arrived nine months earlier, there was a hardness in Crystal's cornflower-blue eyes that bothered me but that was starting to appear less and less. She began to play with dolls and climb trees, finding a childhood she had lost while trying to be her mom's best friend.

I didn't have a lot of patience for Crystal's mom. She was terrible about calling and showing up for visits. When Patty did manage to get around to seeing her daughter, she did little but take Crystal to the mall to hang out. I was a wreck each time Patty took her out. I knew there would be precious little supervision and a lot of exposure to the kind of language and behavior that was just not acceptable for a little girl to hear and see. The plan was for Crystal to be returned to her mom as soon as Patty completed a basic parenting course. That seemed like little enough to ask for, but somehow Patty was unable to achieve it. I was beginning to wonder if Patty was even relieved to be rid of the responsibility of a child so that she could make up for some lost time as an unencumbered teenager.

Jazmine, our second child, was a cherubic three-year-old with skin the color of lightly creamed coffee, a mop of nearly black curls, and almond-shaped eyes. Jazzy, as we all called her, was as plump and roly-poly as a puppy. When she arrived at our house the previous fall, Jazzy had little intelligible speech. All I knew was what I had been told: Jazzy had been found wandering the halls of her apartment building, alone, after ten o'clock at night, wearing nothing but a soppy diaper. When a neighbor brought her home, she found Jazzy's parents drunk in their squalid apartment and completely unaware that their small daughter had slipped out. The neighbor took Jazzy home with her and called social services the next day. When the two social workers assigned to the case knocked on Jazzy's parents' door, they were greeted by the sounds of a loud brawl within. At eleven o'clock in the morning, neither parent had realized that their little girl wasn't home.

Jazzy did well her first few weeks with us. She did have a proclivity for referring to me as a "puckin butch" when she was angry. I was just grateful that her speech was so poor. Hardly anybody else could understand what she was saying. In spite of the name-calling, she seemed to decide early on that I was the mommy. She seldom let me out of her sight for more than a moment, but that's not unusual for a three-year-old. Then the tantrums began. She had several each week, and they were doozies. Jazzy kicked holes in the walls, ripped curtains from the rods, and bit me on more than one occasion.

It would have been so easy to hand in our termination notice on Jazzy, at least in the beginning. I got through many an hour-long tantrum by telling myself that this was it. I had had it with the screaming, and first thing in the morning, I was calling her worker and asking that another home be found for her. But then I would watch her sleeping. I could imagine what it must feel like to be her. To have lived the first three years of your life unsure what the next day or even the next minute would bring. Most of us can't wrap our sheltered minds around the fact that children in our neighborhoods go to bed hungry. We can't accept the reality of the welts a belt makes on the legs of a toddler. Jasmine had no reason to trust me. I would have to earn that trust, and it was going to take time. Lots of time. So morning came and I didn't call. I took a deep breath and faced another day, sure at least that it couldn't be any harder than the day before.

At first I suspected that her tantrums stemmed from Jazzy's inability to use language to process what had happened to her, but the tantrums continued long after Jazzy acquired enough speech to talk about her past. Bruce was inclined to think they happened because of her intense fear of losing us, and indeed they did seem to happen most often at bedtime or when we were going out. Whatever the reason, they were remarkable enough to have me on the phone with a therapist by the end of Jazzy's second month with us.

By some stroke of luck, Andrew Donovan was available to see Jazzy. Andrew had been the therapist for Tyler, one of my earlier foster children, who was also prone to some pretty impressive tantrums. Andrew was a big bear of a man, who countered his size with a sweet, gentle nature and a way of connecting with children that few therapists could match. With his guidance, we were making progress with Jazzy. As her speech improved, she began to relate some of what had gone on in her birth home. It was clear that this little girl had long been the victim of some pretty significant abuse at the hands of both of her parents. Some of the abuse bordered on the sadistic, and I never felt we should rule out sexual abuse as well. Just because a kid doesn't have the language to give you the details doesn't mean it didn't happen. Neither of Jazzy's parents was prepared to take parenting or anger management classes, and they weren't willing to address their problems with alcohol. All of this was necessary before social services would begin to consider sending their child home. When it was discovered that both of Jazzy's parents had lost children from previous relationships to social services in other states, Jazzy's social worker submitted the paperwork to the legal department to have the case moved to the adoption unit. After eighteen months with us, Jazzy was being assigned an adoption worker. A trial date to terminate Jazzy's parents' parental rights had already been scheduled.

As the months dragged on, I considered adopting Jazzy myself. Bruce and I spent hours discussing the pros and cons. Certainly, any move was going to be hard on this child, and only a very special family was going to have the stamina to see her through such a transition. But there were other things to think about. We had finalized the adoption of our youngest daughter, Karen, only a year earlier. Since we had six children to educate, and given our ages, forty-six and fifty-two, taking on a three-year-old with major tantrums seemed like a bit much. Still, every time Jazzy wrapped her pudgy brown arms around my neck and whispered, "I yuv you, Mamma," my resolve threatened to crumble. It is the tragedy of doing the kind of long-term foster care that Bruce and I did. Broken hearts are inevitable. We were grown-ups and knew what we were getting into, but our foster children had no choice in the matter.

This kind of emotional dilemma made me understand why some families chose to keep some distance in their relationships with the children they care for. It is certainly less painful that way, but it never worked for me. I'm from the better-to-have-loved-and-lost school. Children need to be cared for by some-one who lights up when they walk into a room. Kids can recover from loss. What they can't recover from is feeling invisible.

Our third little girl was a cute, slightly overweight ten-year-old of Puerto Rican descent named Priscilla. She had been with us for nearly a year, and I confess to not always being particularly fond of her.

Priscilla had first come to us as a hotline placement. She was one of those kids who had been in and out of care for years. Her parents both suffered from pretty extreme mental illness. When they took their medication, they were good parents. But most psychiatric medications have unpleasant side effects. They can cause weight gain, drowsiness, and tremors. A lot of people just can't tolerate them. Priscilla's parents would take their medication until they had recovered enough to regain custody of their daughter, but once she was home, they would get sloppy about it. After a few months they would stop taking their pills entirely. Almost simultaneously, they would go into crisis and need to be hospitalized. Priscilla would then come back into care.

The moves were tough on Priscilla. At home she ruled the roost and was in danger of becoming a real tyrant. She didn't do much besides read and eat junk food. Each time she went to a foster home, she was a bit more difficult than the time before. The behaviors weren't dramatic, just wearing. Priscilla was a tattletale and a whiner, who had to run the show. She had to pick the games and decide on the rules. If she didn't get her own way, she pouted and sulked until my more compliant children gave in and let her have what she wanted. She made a point of showing off an expensive gift from her father just when Crystal's mother had forgotten Crystal's birthday. Behavior like that didn't endear her to the rest of the household, and more and more often, I found myself running interference over unimportant squabbles. I hated that role, especially since I had to fight with myself to remain fair. Sometimes the other kids really were unkind to Priscilla, but it was hard for me to drum up much sympathy when, so often, it felt as if she was asking for it.

Still, as with all of my children, there was that vulnerability that lurked below the surface, even in the toughest of them. Priscilla pined for her parents. She was particularly close to her father, an intelligent man who spent hours reading to Priscilla and teaching her about everything from botany to astronomy. At ten Priscilla was a fluent reader and years ahead of her classmates in math. The other kids admired her talents, but at recess, while they ran off to play soccer and tag, Priscilla was left to sit by herself on the sidelines.

When Priscilla returned from a visit, the pain in her eyes could move me to tears. No child should have to be that sad. I knew that pain was the cause of her attitude, and that fact kept me hanging in with her in spite of how often she pushed my emotional buttons. After a year Priscilla was becoming more likable. She was beginning to understand that the rules at her home were not the same as the rules at my house. She didn't like it, but she was learning to cope.

In addition to these three girls, Bruce and I still had three of our five older children still living at home. At fourteen, seventeen, and eighteen, Angie, Neddy, and Ben were in high school and busy with all that entailed. Our adopted four-year-old daughter, Karen, spent her time with the younger crew. Altogether, even with Jazzy's tantrums and Priscilla's attitude problem, this was the easiest group of children we had ever parented, and Bruce and I were enjoying every minute of it.

Many friends and more than a few of our relatives questioned the wisdom of the decision Bruce and I had made to provide temporary and sometimes not-so-temporary care to a gaggle of troubled little girls, but we no longer even debated it. We loved what we did. We loved the feeling we got from doing something with our lives that mattered. We loved the intensity and the unpredictability. We loved the chance we had to make a better life for children, and we loved our little girls.

By the end of the day, Crystal, Jazzy, and Priscilla were moved into their new room. I tucked a final stack of pajamas into a drawer, straightened the books on Jazzy's dresser, and looked around with a small sigh. I felt a familiar stirring, a sense of expectancy. I knew it wouldn't lift until the one empty bed in the farthest corner of the room was filled.

Two

I had that indefinable something referred to by social workers as "experience." What that meant was that I had been providing care to children for more than the six months that many families new to foster care last, and that I tended to stick it out with some pretty disturbed kids. As a consequence, I received a lot of calls about kids who were considered hard to place. That suited me just fine. Although I had enjoyed the relative calmness in the house, I was also feeling restless, unchallenged. I knew what I was missing. It was the odd jolt of excitement I felt when working with a kid who just refused to try to pass for normal. I am fascinated by the myriad ways traumatized children learn to cope within a world that makes no sense. What looks like crazy can be the sanest thing imaginable when you know how a child has lived. Child abuse can be an isolated case of a spanking that got out of hand. Neglect can be more about poverty and despair than a disregard for the needs of your child. But it can be, and often is, about unspeakable horror. I knew children who had lived their lives in a technicolor nightmare. I took care of kids with broken bones and cigarette burns. My children had police records and venereal disease.

But my kids had other things. I have known young children willing to sacrifice their own safety in order to protect younger brothers and sisters. I remember a little girl who, after telling me about being raped by an uncle, then spent the next hour fashioning a handmade birthday card for Bruce. It was pretty amazing stuff, and it made me glad every day that I had found the courage to leave the relative safety of a classroom for the gritty reality of foster parenting.

Over the next week I turned down a couple of children who needed placement but hadn't seemed like good matches for our family. There was a pregnant fifteen-year-old, who certainly needed the support of a stable family, but I thought it might be hard for her to share a room with Angie, who was the same age but whose concerns went little beyond her next Spanish exam and getting ready for spring soccer tryouts. The three-year-old with developmental delays would have been perfect, but she had court-ordered visits with her mother twice a week and there was no way for my schedule to accommodate that. Still, as days passed without a call for a child to fill my empty bed, I began to regret my decision to turn down that little one. When a foster parenting friend called to tell me about the six-year-old twins she was getting that afternoon, I sulked for the rest of the day. When a full week went by, I was beginning to feel a bit ghoulish in my pining for another child. After all, the only way for me to have what I wanted was for another family to sink into the mire of social services. Although the goal of foster care is to provide temporary shelter for children until their family can be safely re-unified, the reality for a lot of kids is somewhat different. One in five children who enter foster care won't go home again. Some will return home to situations that are essentially unchanged. Others may return home for a while but find themselves back in care many more times before they reach adulthood. Years of having their children bounce around in foster care leaves many families not just broken but shattered and beyond repair. After endless meetings and reams of paperwork, all that is left of too many families is a summary in someone's unread file. I was still coming to terms with the notion of building my life around other people's misery.

We had a standing joke in our foster parent support group: If you need a quiet weekend, don't answer the phone after four on Friday afternoon. Workers who have watched their assigned families fall apart all week often decide that the kids won't be safe over the weekend and then request emergency placement. A lot of people must have wanted a quiet weekend, because when the phone finally rang for me on that second Friday in January, it was already nearly five and the home-finding worker sounded panicked.

"Hey, Kathy, I hope you can help me out. I've got a waiting

room full of teens to place and I just got handed three more requests for beds for younger kids."

I bristled a bit at my house being referred to as a bed, as though there were no people living here.

"Tell me about them."

I could hear the sounds of paper being shuffled and faint screams from the background. "Let's see. I've got the youngest Matthews girl, Tiffany. She's not quite four. I think you had her older sister for a few weeks last year."

"I thought those girls were with an aunt."

"They were, but there have been some ongoing problems. The day care facility has been complaining that Tiffany is coming in hungry and dirty, and this week she had a couple of suspicious bruises. The aunt sounded pretty relieved when we called her on it. I think this has been more than she bargained for. Anyway, Tiffany is adorable. She has no special needs and no medical issues. I also have a ten-year-old. Carmen Santiago. Her mom just got sentenced to three months in jail for writing bad checks. Dad has a drug problem, so we can't leave her home. Carmen has hearing aids but no other special needs. She's in an honors program in school. Very bright little girl. Then I've got Daisy, but I think we may need to find a hotline bed for her this weekend and look for a specialized slot next week."

My curiosity got the best of me. "Why? What's up with her?"

"Only six but two prior psych hospitalizations. Anorexic. Aggressive toward her mother. Very little speech. Maybe retarded. Very depressed. She's on a ton of medication."

"Poor kid. Families won't be lining up to take on that kind of work."

"That's for sure. I hope specialized will have something for her."

It took a moment for the pictures to organize themselves in my mind.

I knew Tiffany slightly. She was cute and bubbly, one of a large clan of kids who all bounced around the foster care system long enough for their names to be familiar with foster parents. Tiffany was still young and in pretty good shape. She would be a great fit with Karen and Jazzy. I liked what I was hearing about Carmen. If she had battled a tough home life and a hearing loss and still managed to hold her own in an honors program, she certainly had some good stuff going on. And she could be good for Priscilla and Crystal. The handwriting was on the wall for Daisy. If specialized couldn't come up with something for her, she was headed for a residential treatment program somewhere. I was leaning toward taking Carmen since I was hoping for an older kid. I just wished that Bruce was home so I could hear his opinion.

"Hey! Are you still there?"

"Sorry." I laughed. "I'm just thinking. Tiffany and Carmen sound like they'll be easy to place, so I guess it will be Daisy. I'd like to take Daisy."

I have no idea where the hubris came from that offered to take Daisy, but whatever confidence I had diminished considerably between that phone call and the knock on the door that signaled Daisy's arrival. We were a family that constantly re-created itself. Every new arrival changed the dynamics and not always for the better. We had, in the past, cared for some very disturbed children. It had been hard on all of us. Bruce had been very clear. He wanted us to be a family, not a hospital. He was unlikely to be enthusiastic about a child who couldn't function in a family setting. We wanted to be able to have fun with our children, and we wanted to make a difference in their lives. We had learned from the bitter experience of caring for two children we couldn't help that love is not always enough to change the outcome for a child. I didn't have any information about Daisy beyond what I had heard on the phone, but it was enough for me to know that something was very wrong with this little girl and caring for her wasn't going to be easy.

The call for Daisy had come so late that social services had opted to leave her at home until the following morning. That meant placing her on a weekend, which wasn't usual. It came about only because her ongoing worker happened to be working the hotline. The entire odd placement should have been a sign. But the delay at least gave me a chance to prepare Bruce for Daisy's arrival.

"I thought we weren't going to do this anymore, Kathy."

"Do what? Give kids a chance before we wrote them off?"

"No. Take on more than we can handle. This kid sounds like a bottomless pit of need. Where are you going to find the hours for the doctors and the therapist and the academics? We have seven other kids who need us. Somebody's going to lose out."

That Bruce was right didn't help my attitude.

"Let's just give it a try for the weekend. If it doesn't work, we can call on Monday. It's only two days, and she's barely six. How hard can it be?"

Our conversation was interrupted by a crash and a chorus of screams from the playroom.

Bruce headed up the stairs with a backward glance. "Gee, honey, I don't know. How hard can it be?"

I spent a sleepless night wondering how I would manage with Daisy and a busy morning preparing for her arrival. I didn't say much to the girls except that we were expecting a child and that I wanted all of them to remember how it felt to be new and scared. I wanted to see everybody's best self, I told them. Most children love to have an opportunity to show kindness; mine were no exception. They all scurried around helping me make up Daisy's bed with clean sheets and finding some stuffed animals to share with her.

When Daisy arrived on Saturday afternoon, she didn't walk in the front door. She scuttled. Like a small crab, she sidled away from me, making only brief eye contact and refusing to respond to my forced attempts at friendliness. She ignored the girls, too. They had gathered in the kitchen, chatting away, each wanting to be the first to claim the new girl as a friend. They were silenced and, I think, a bit frightened by Daisy's aloofness. She flitted from one piece of furniture, one toy, one book to the next, examining each only briefly before moving on. Nothing held her attention for more than a moment until she spied our cat, Molly. Daisy squealed with something akin to pleasure and grabbed the cat, clutching her too tightly around the stomach. Molly struggled to get loose, but Daisy seemed oblivious of the cat's discomfort.

"Molly doesn't like to be held so tightly, honey. It hurts her. Put her down and pet her gently. Like this." Daisy let me take Molly from her and even let me run her hand gently over the cat's rumpled fur. "There you go. Molly will like you if you're kind to her."

I took the few minutes that Daisy spent stroking Molly to get a better look at her. What struck me was how unwell she looked. Her dark hair was so thin and wispy that in places her scalp showed through. There was not an ounce of fat on her emaciated body. Thin ribbons of green mucus ran from her nose. Dark eyes were sunk deep in her skull. I wondered when she had last eaten a real meal. She could not have been called pretty; she was anything but—however, there was an innocence about her that I found appealing.

I needed to do something to connect with Daisy, to establish myself as the mother and this place as home. For most kids, I offer comfort food. Bread puddings and thick soups. Toast with lots of melted butter and hot chocolate. But given the trouble Daisy was reported to have with food, I thought it best to offer something a little less intimidating.

"Are you thirsty, Daisy? Would you like some juice?"

"Nuh, nuh, nuh! I no wanna." Daisy waved her hands in the air as if to ward off an attack. Her speech was nearly unintelligible. I could see why retardation had been suggested.

"You aren't thirsty now. Maybe you'll want something

later." If Daisy heard me, she gave no sign. She flapped her arms a few times, then dropped to the floor and began to rock. I turned to her social worker, Evelyn, and inclined my head toward the living room. I wanted to talk without Daisy at my feet.

Evelyn was a tall birdlike woman with huge glasses and a habit of talking and moving at the same time. She was apologizing before we sat down.

"I'm sorry to do this to you, Kathy. Do you think you can get through the weekend?"

"That shouldn't be a problem. She looks too sick to be dangerous. What the heck is going on with this kid? I know she has some food issues, and I was told she doesn't talk."

Evelyn gave an elaborate shrug of her shoulders and shifted around on the sofa. "I was told the same thing. Apparently, she didn't talk while she was in the hospital, although her mother says she talks at home."

"What about the food issues? She certainly looks anorexic, but it's hard to believe a kid this young will really refuse to eat unless there's something physically wrong with her."

"According to her mother, Daisy will drink water and she'll eat dry cereal and applesauce. Pretty much everything else will make her gag and sometimes actually vomit."

I was beginning to feel a bit discouraged. "I suppose she's been checked out medically."

"Every test known to man," Evelyn replied. "We have a long list of what she doesn't have but no idea about what she does have, besides a laundry list of psychiatric problems."

"Do I dare ask what they might be?"

"Let's see," said Evelyn, fumbling around in her briefcase for her paperwork. "Posttraumatic stress disorder. Attention deficit with hyperactivity disorder. Generalized anxiety disorder. Multiple phobias. Oppositional defiant disorder. Daisy's mom, Glenna, gave me the meds and a schedule of when they need to be given. I have it here someplace." Evelyn fumbled through her briefcase and finally pulled out a crumpled envelope. "Maybe you can figure this out. It makes no sense to me."

I wasn't surprised that Evelyn couldn't understand the directions for Daisy's medications. They were filled with qualifiers like "If she'll take it," "If she seems to need it," and "Should be given twice a day, but she won't swallow it." The whole thing was further complicated because I didn't recognize the names of several of the drugs, and the directions on the bottles were different from the ones her mother sent.

"I can't do this, Evelyn," I said firmly. "It's not safe. It looks like she hasn't had any of this stuff consistently for the last couple of weeks. If I do manage to get all of it into her, she's likely to be snowed. Her body isn't used to it."

"I can't authorize you to stop her meds without a doctor's order. The physician's name is on the bottle. If you can reach her and get the okay, well, that's up to her. Otherwise, you'll have to give it to her. I can understand how you feel. It is a lot of medication."

I will confess that medicating children for what often seems like pretty good adaptive responses to a crummy home life annoys me. A lot of the medication being prescribed for children in the late 1990s was designed for adults, not children with developing brains. There wasn't much research out there on the long-term effects, and what there was wasn't usually available to the general public. Even the diagnostic labels are open to interpretation. What is hyperactivity, anyway? Is it a problem for the child or for the adults who care for him? How do you distinguish between anxiety that is caused by environment and anxiety caused by faulty brain wiring? Shouldn't calm and predictable reactions to challenging behavior be the first line of treatment for an oppositional kid, or is it just easier on everyone to slip him a pill? It was discouraging to see so many kids come to the door with a prescription for Ritalin but not the name of a therapist they could talk to.

The pill answer is not always as simple as it seems. If a family's resources are worn down, it may be necessary to use medication as a means of keeping everybody together enough to function. And certainly, if any kid looked like a candidate for medication, Daisy was one.

"What's the deal with the posttraumatic stress diagnosis?" I asked.

Evelyn looked surprised. "Didn't home-finding tell you that Daisy may have been sexually abused?"

I thought of that thin little waif with the hungry eyes and felt a familiar surge of white-hot anger.

"May have been? You aren't sure?"

"I guess she drew some suggestive pictures while she was hospitalized, and she played out some sexual stuff with some dolls in therapy. The clinician who worked with her wasn't sure how serious it was or what its impact was on her, or even if it really happened. Daisy isn't exactly a barrel of information."

"Home-finding didn't mention it. Who do they think might have done it?"

"Daisy didn't say, but she hasn't had a lot of contact with anybody except a boyfriend of her mom's. He lived with Glenna and Daisy for at least the last four years. Glenna says she had no idea he might have been hurting Daisy until after she got out of the hospital a couple of weeks ago, and she still isn't sure. She doesn't see how it could have happened without her knowing about it. It's to her credit though that she kicked the guy out. A lot of women keep abusers around even after they find out."

"Is there a dad in the picture?"

"Glenna won't talk about him. I don't think he's been around for years. Mom is a bit out there. She spends a lot of time talking about karma and energy fields. I don't think she's unkind. Just disconnected. There's a grandmother who's an attorney. She's involved but too busy to be much help. I think she probably pays the bills. Glenna waits tables in a coffeehouse over by the college on the weekends, but I don't think she makes much money. She refused to take a drug screen, if that tells you anything."

"What's the plan here? It sounds like this could be one of those go-nowhere cases."

"It looks like Daisy will need a residential treatment placement eventually or, at the very least, a specialized slot. Mom may just need time to process what she's heard and figure out how to help her kid. She certainly doesn't feel up to caring for Daisy. She requested a placement right after Daisy was released from the hospital. If Daisy really is as disturbed as she looks now, we'll have to help Glenna explore the options for a specialized placement. We've actually got a place in mind already."

"I don't get it," I said, puzzled by this story. "If Mom even suspects that her kid has been molested, how can she just send her away? She should be devastated, sure, but instinct ought to have kicked in. I can't believe she can let this kid out of her sight, forget about sending her to live with strangers. It doesn't add up."

Evelyn gave me a wry little smile.

"You're a foster parent and you expect the world to make sense? Sorry, hon, but you've gone into the wrong line of work."

I was glad to have Evelyn leave so that I could return to Daisy. Karen and Jazzy had gone upstairs to play, and Priscilla and Crystal were already in the mudroom grabbing snowsuits and hats. Usually, a new child is the center of attention while everybody gets to know her, but it was clear that Daisy was a disappointment to the older girls. Karen and Jazzy were okay playmates for dolls and blocks, but they were still in preschool and not very good at following rules. Priscilla and Crystal were hoping for a more competent child to make their games of tag and hide-and-seek more interesting. Poor Daisy was anything but competent-looking. I don't think it occurred to them to ask her to join them outside.

Alone now, Daisy stood in the center of the kitchen. She flapped her hands and rocked from side to side, giggling to herself. I felt a brief moment of panic. I had no idea where to start with this child. I wasn't a doctor or a special education teacher or a lawyer or a therapist or any of the other people Daisy needed right now. Mostly, I wasn't her mother, which was the one thing I suspected she needed most.

"Hey, Daisy," I said with a brightness I didn't feel. "Come and help me sort your clothes."

Daisy looked at me with a sweet little smile and hopped over to where I was standing. Both the smile and the response were unexpected, and I felt a familiar little tug I recognized as hope.

"Mine?"

"Yes, sweetie, these are your things. Can you help me take them out of your suitcase?"

The suitcase itself was unusual. Most of my kids come with their clothes tossed into green garbage bags—that's if they come with anything at all. Not only did Daisy have a suitcase, but she had an expensive suitcase, and it was packed with some very nice clothes and new socks, underwear, and pajamas. I recognized the brands as ones I couldn't afford unless I found them in a secondhand store. Most of the children who come to me have lived in families where poverty is a constant companion. Dresses from Land's End and Hanna Andersson T-shirts are not in the budget. Everything Daisy had was clean and neatly folded.

Sorting took only a few minutes. I wasn't sure what to expect when I gave a pile of clothes to Daisy and asked her to carry it upstairs. She was reported to be oppositional. I wouldn't have

been at all surprised at any response except, perhaps, the one
that I got.

"Okay. I help. I help. Okay?"

The words were hard to understand, but her face was easy to
read. Daisy looked up at me with what I can only call an angelic
little smile. There was something otherworldly about her, a
sense of not being from the same galaxy as the rest of us. With
the other children out from underfoot, Daisy seemed calmer and
better able to attend. When I first met her, I thought Daisy
seemed nearly autistic with her flapping and spinning. Now, on
closer examination, it was more that she wasn't quite sure how
to connect or what was likely to happen next. Given the unpredictability of her past few months, with moves from home to
hospital to home to me, that was understandable. And if her
mother's boyfriend had really abused her, she had no reason to
trust a strange adult either.

I wanted to touch Daisy. It was one of the reasons I left teaching for foster care. In the classroom, there was always the need to
remember my place on the periphery of a child's life. It wasn't
enough for me. I wanted to get close to children, to have relationships that weren't destined to end each June. At that moment, I wanted to do some little Mommy thing for Daisy. I still
longed to feed her, but I didn't want to rush things. There was
no hurry. I settled for taking both of her thin hands in mine.

"Your nose is running, hon. Let's wash your face. Okay?"

I led Daisy to the bathroom and gently cleaned her face with
a soft, old washcloth. Daisy flinched when I got near her face, a

small movement that made me cringe, but she let me clean her. I knelt down to look at her and held up a hand mirror so she could see herself. Daisy looked at her image for a long time and then smiled at me.

"You look so pretty, Daisy. Let's put some tissue in your pocket. When your nose runs, you can wipe it with that instead of your hand. Okay?"

Daisy nodded. She started to spin and flap her hands again. I stood behind her, wrapped my arms around her bony frame, and whispered in her ear.

"Take a deep breath, sweetie. Hey, did you know that I have the best job in the whole world? My job is to keep kids safe. I get to make sure things aren't so scary. Bad things won't happen to you here. Okay?"

Daisy rocked from side to side then turned to face me and looked steadily into my eyes. There was something unnerving in her frank appraisal of me. After a moment she looked away and took my hand in hers. We took her clothes and went upstairs together, Daisy pasted to my side like she was Velcroed there.

I brought Daisy to the littles' room, pointing out who slept where as we went along. Karen and Jazzy were already there, playing with the dollhouse. Daisy dropped her clothes, let out a squeal, and rushed toward them. Karen's eyes widened in fear. Karen was a funny little girl about any number of things, but chief among them was a horror of things being out of place. The dollhouse furniture was set up just the way Karen liked it, ordered and symmetrical.

"Wait, Daisy," I said while pulling her back to me. "Let's

walk over quietly. Can you ask the girls if they want to play? They'll feel better about letting you play if you're careful of their things."

Daisy looked confused, so I led her to the dollhouse.

"This is Karen and this is Jazzy. Girls, this is Daisy. I think she wants to play, too."

Karen took the lead. "You can play, but don't mess things up. You can be the brother."

How generous, I thought with a smile. The new girl gets stuck with the part nobody else wants. But I underestimated Daisy. She answered with unexpected clarity.

"No. I baby. I wanna be baby."

Daisy knelt next to Jazzy and grabbed the baby from its place in the cradle. "Momma. Momma," she cried with a high-pitched, grating voice.

Ignoring the other two children, Daisy surveyed the wooden house. Very deliberately, she picked up one of the mommy dolls. Slowly, almost painfully, she moved her from her place in the kitchen to an upstairs bedroom. She paused there, holding the doll aloft, then moved her to the far corner, facing the wall.

"Can't hear you. Can't hear you," she whispered softly.

She next moved the father doll to the living room. Daisy seemed to ponder his placement for a very long time before deciding where he belonged. She sat him on the sofa with his feet stretched out before him. With no wasted movements, Daisy began to pile extra furniture and doll clothes on him until he was completely buried. Karen started to protest, but I pulled her onto my lap, shaking my head slightly. Whatever Daisy was doing was important to her, and I didn't want to interrupt. Daisy picked up the baby doll again. This time there was no hesitation. She placed the baby back in the cradle, and then turned it upside down, trapping the baby underneath. She heaved a deep sigh and muttered something that sounded like "All gone," and sat back on her heels.

It was a strange little scenario. It upset me, although I couldn't really say why. Lots of children had used our dollhouse to act out far more brutal events, but there was something unusual about the way Daisy acted. I thought there was some message here I was supposed to get that was lost on me.

With her small drama over, Daisy seemed content to play alongside, if not exactly with, Karen and Jazzy. Since a couple of the teenagers were around to listen in on the little girls, I was free to go downstairs and contemplate my next move.

The girls were accustomed to an afternoon snack, and I wasn't sure what to do about it. I was tempted to let Daisy skip the whole thing, given the extent of her food issues. But, in general, I had found that avoidance was not the best strategy for helping my kids learn to cope. We all ate, and Daisy was going to have to eat, too. I had some hope that if I just set the food out and acted as if I expected her to eat, she would eat and the problem would be solved. Of course, it wasn't that easy.

I searched the cabinets, looking for something to fix that was reasonably healthy but with certain kid appeal. I settled on blueberry muffins and apple slices and added a small bowl of cream cheese to the table. I even went so far as to put out the cloth napkins and holiday mugs. It was the kind of special touch that I didn't always take the time for, but I wanted the table to look inviting. Since the day was so cold, I made a pot of hot chocolate.

I called Priscilla and Crystal in first. They tumbled in from their outside play, apple-cheeked and ravenous. The younger crowd heard the commotion and raced to the table before I called them. Daisy came in behind the others. She stood in the doorway of the kitchen, watching as the girls helped themselves to muffins and cream cheese and piled mounds of snowy whipped cream on their cups of steaming chocolate. Her breathing changed as she watched them, each breath quicker and deeper than the one before. It took me a moment to realize that she was hyperventilating.

"Hey, sweetie. Time to calm down, okay? I need you to slow your breaths down. Can you watch me and breathe like I do? Slow, baby. Slow down."

I used my calmest voice and talked very softly, the way one would to a skittish kitten, and led her to the table. Once again the innate kindness of my girls surfaced quickly. Priscilla moved over and motioned for Daisy to take her seat. This placed Daisy between the two older girls. Such a move may not seem like a big deal, but children who live in foster homes often have very little to call their own. Their place at the table matters to them. It signifies ownership and belonging. For Priscilla to make that offer spoke to what a generous little girl was hiding underneath her difficult exterior.

Crystal reached over and placed a muffin on Daisy's plate and handed her a napkin. The sight of the muffin was too much for Daisy. She began to rock back and forth in her chair. I could hear her count from one to ten, faintly, over and over again in a soft, lispy whisper.

It occurred to me that a whole muffin was probably too much to start with. I moved Daisy's plate to the side and bent down next to her.

"I'll bet food can be a little scary when you haven't eaten for a while. Let's start with something smaller. How about one slice of apple?"

Daisy looked as if she was going to cry. Her eyes filled up and her bottom lip quivered. She looked so pathetic, with her snotty nose and pinched-up little face, that I nearly gave in and told her to get up. But I didn't want her first time at the table to end with failure for her or for me.

"Come on, Daisy. One slice of apple and we'll find something fun to do. Do you like Muppets? I have a Muppet movie we could put on when you're done."

Daisy kept her jaw clamped shut, and I felt myself stiffen at what, at first glance, seemed like her stubbornness. I was kept from impatience by two thoughts. The first was that in any control battle with a kid over food, one way or the other, the kid is going to win. The second was that Daisy didn't look oppositional. She looked scared, and if she was, there was probably a good reason for it. That softened me enough to try another tactic.

"I heard that you like applesauce, Daisy. Did you know that applesauce is nothing but mushed-up apples? Look! You can make applesauce yourself. Take the fork and push down real hard."

I put the fork in Daisy's hand and helped her mash up a slice of apple. It didn't make much sauce. But the other girls were impressed, and of course, they had to mash up their apples, too. Soon everyone was scooping up sloppy spoonfuls of homemade applesauce. Amid the chorus of giggles, Daisy managed to swallow a couple of bites.

It's amazing how a little success feeds upon itself. After I got the girls settled with a Muppet movie, I popped a big bowl of buttery, salty popcorn and set it up on the coffee table in the den along with a pitcher of orange juice and the plastic margarita glasses I had stashed away at the end of the summer. I didn't say anything. I just put everything out and hoped Daisy would see everyone else eating and drinking while watching the movie and decide to join them. What she didn't need, I was certain, was the pressure of thinking that each time food was presented she needed to prepare herself for war.

After the movie I counted out the three pills Daisy was supposed to take. I tried hiding them in ice cream, which she wouldn't eat, and I attempted a firmness I wasn't sure I really felt. On this issue, Daisy wouldn't budge. She wasn't taking those pills and that was final. If I had known as much about psychiatric medications then as I do now, I would have been a lot more concerned. Psychiatric medications are tricky things and not something one can afford to be cavalier about. They need to be taken consistently and on time. This is a child's brain chemistry we're fooling around with. As it was, after fifteen minutes of prodding on my part and refusal on Daisy's, I gave up and put her meds in the locked tackle box I kept on top of the refrigerator. I put in a call to the physician listed on the prescription bottle and left a message for her to return my call. This was one problem I was quite happy to be able to hand off to someone else.

I called Bruce at work, too. I wanted to give him a heads-up about the possibility of sexual abuse. We had cared for a depressing number of little girls who had been sexually abused. While some children show the panic of a trapped animal when a man comes near, others react with provocative flirting. The saddest for me are the ones who have shut down, escaping mentally because they have learned there is no other way out.

I needn't have worried about Daisy. She greeted Bruce with the same kind of spacey little smile and flapping and spinning as she had greeted the rest of us. The smile seemed to touch him. He reached out to smooth the hair back from her face and smiled back at her.

"Hello, Daisy. It's nice to have you with us."

Daisy didn't answer, but she did sidle up next to him and just barely lay her head against his hip. It was a sweet gesture, made more sweet because it was so unexpected.

I had prepared what I hoped was a fairly inoffensive dinner. You can't get much more bland than chicken breasts, rice, and peas. Still, Daisy couldn't manage more than a few grains of rice. The question of whether to give in and let her eat dry cereal weighed on me. I didn't want to make the eating problem worse by being too quick to offer an alternative, especially one that was woefully inadequate as far as nutrition went, but I didn't want to make meals the power struggle I suspected they were at home, either. In the end, I gave her a bowl of cereal, not because I thought it was best but just because I had no better idea.

Bedtime at my house was often a disaster. Neither Crystal nor Priscilla had ever had an established bedtime before coming to live with us. Crystal, in particular, was quite used to catching David Letterman on TV while she waited up for her mother, and both girls tried every way possible to keep from turning in at what they considered to be an unreasonable hour. Jazzy still threw major tantrums many nights. I often sent the older girls to bed down in the den, while I tried to get Jazzy to settle down in an effort to spare them the worst of her screaming. I hoped for one of Jazzy's rare compliant nights on Daisy's first night with us, but with a new child in the house, that wasn't to be. Jazzy was screaming before we even reached the stairs. That left Neddy to deal with Daisy, no one thinking it was a good idea to have Bruce dress Daisy in her pajamas. I went through the usual routine of rocking Jazzy for a few minutes, putting her in bed, then talking softly while I eased myself out the door. It seldom went as smoothly as it sounds. Many nights I had to leave with her howling. Those were actually the good nights. On a bad night she wouldn't stay in her bed or her room, and I could spend an hour putting her back to bed over and over. I have to admit that on more than a few nights I called a foster parenting friend and asked her to talk to me while Jazzy screamed in the background, so I wouldn't lose my temper and do something I would later regret. I wasn't tempted to spank her, but I was certainly tempted to really yell, and there was never any doubt that yelling wasn't the answer here.

This was one of those long nights when the only solution was to lie in bed with Jazzy until she fell asleep. I must have dozed off myself, because when I woke the room was dark and the other girls were all in bed. I could make out Neddy's voice singing softly. I realized she was lying with Daisy and singing her to sleep. I smiled in the dark. Neddy was unusually good with all of the children, but she was a teenager and had given up valuable phone time to help Daisy settle down.

Once both little girls were sleeping soundly, Neddy and I went downstairs together. We were going through a difficult time with Neddy that year. Adolescence is tough for many families, and ours was not immune. The complications of adoption and foster care and racial and cultural identity made a hard time even worse. Bruce and I were constantly clashing with Neddy over curfews and limits on phone time, and homework or lack thereof. Still, underneath the tough exterior of a hostile adolescent, Neddy was a good kid and she really cared about our little ones.

"What is there about this kid, Mom?" Neddy asked quietly. "She's a little odd, but she's kind of sweet."

That was the only word for Daisy. Sweet. Sweetness is an unusual quality for kids in foster care. Abuse, neglect, poverty, the soul-wrenching sadness of not having parents who can love you often rob children of their sweetness. But not so with Daisy. In spite of the gloomy diagnoses and the very obvious problems, underneath was one of the sweetest little girls any of us had ever run across. Strange little Daisy was a keeper.

Bruce and I sat up for a late-night cup of coffee. We talked
about Jazzy's tantrums and Crystal's mother's upcoming visit.
Bruce was wondering if there was a connection between Neddy's
rebellion and the subsequent friction it caused and Karen's increasing anxiety. Karen had lived with us from the time she was
a baby. She had never had another placement and had never suffered from any unusual trauma. When we adopted her at age
three, she was the picture of health, physically and psychologi-
cally. But over the past few months, things had changed for
Karen. She was still healthy, never even getting a cold, but she
had recently developed several tics. She had been blinking her
eyes and wiggling her nose for several weeks and had just added
a constant sniff to her repertoire. Then there was the increasing
problem with control issues. Things needed to be not just in
order but symmetrical. She liked things to match and be even,
right down to the length of her shoelaces and the pillows on her
bed. Frankly, we were worried and not at all sure what we should
do about this. Karen was scheduled for a physical in March, and
since there was nothing about her behavior that suggested a crisis, we agreed to wait to speak to her pediatrician then.

The talk finally came around to Daisy. Bruce was already
convinced that even with hospitalizations, the plan for a specialized placement was all wrong.

"I think of those places as being for kids who are so difficult
that they aren't safe to be around or for kids who might hurt
themselves. Daisy may be odd, but she doesn't seem like she's a
safety problem."

"She has a history of hitting her mother."

"You haven't met her mother. Maybe she needs hitting."

"Very funny, dear. I like Daisy a lot, but do we have to think about this? You're the one who said she might not be right for us. We really don't need an aggressive kid when Karen seems so fragile. This could just be a honeymoon."

"Let's let her be innocent until proven otherwise. It wouldn't be the first time a kid turns out to be totally different from what we were told she was like. If there is any way to keep her out of a residential program, we owe it to her to try."

I smiled in the dark. It had taken only one evening for Bruce to have a change of heart about Daisy. That probably said as much about Bruce as it did about Daisy.

I gave a sigh. "It isn't our call anyway. She's already on the list for a slot in specialized foster care. And don't forget, this is a voluntary placement. Her mother gets to decide what happens."

"We've had kids on the list before. It can take months. And if she does well here, maybe her mother won't insist. Not once she's seen what those places are like. Boarding school, they ain't."

Bruce was right. Residential facilities are designed for kids who are so out of control that they need the kind of rules that make these places look more like prisons than schools. Daisy would get eaten alive in a place like that.

Three

Evelyn didn't have a problem with our wanting to keep Daisy as a permanent placement and neither did Daisy's mother, although she was apparently baffled by our decision. There was an unusual request, though, and one I felt a little offended by. Evelyn asked if Glenna and her mother could come by to meet me and see Daisy's room. They had heard all of the foster parent horror stories and wanted to be sure that Daisy was in a safe place.

I knew the picture they had painted in their heads. At best, we would be indifferent caretakers in the business for the money and unconcerned with the needs of the children entrusted to us. At worst, we would be the family in the newspapers. The one who gained notoriety after starving a baby or keeping their foster children in cages. It is undoubtedly the same picture I would have painted a few years earlier. In fact, I knew of a few foster homes I wouldn't have wished on any kid. But that begged the question: If Glenna was so worried about Daisy's safety, why had she requested a voluntary placement to begin with? I knew any number of families with no resources who fought tooth and nail to keep their children from being placed in foster care. I agreed to let her visit, but I wasn't happy about it. While I did allow some parents to pick up their children at my house, I agreed to it only when I had met them at the office several times and could be certain that they would not pose a threat to my family. I really didn't like feeling as though I was being evaluated by a parent. It was the department's job to make sure that I was doing my job and that my home was safe, not the parents', and I had never heard of social services making such a demand before. I didn't want to think that Glenna was getting special treatment because of her family's social status, but it did feel that way.

In spite of my reservations, Glenna was coming. At ten o'clock on the following Tuesday morning, I found myself checking over the house, wondering how it would look through the eyes of a stranger.

I love my house. I love the funny, sloped ceilings and the odd corners and cupboards, but I knew that by most standards it was shabby and clearly showed the effects of eight kids running in and out all day. Our art consisted mainly of the stuff on the refrigerator that the kids brought home from school. The mudroom deserved its name, and the kitchen sink was never empty. I tried to keep things neat, but there always seemed to be a science project on the dining room table and snowsuits thawing in the bathtub. Still, it was a warm, homey place, and on that crisp morning, with the sun slanting across the living room floor, I thought it looked lovely.

Evelyn arrived her usual fifteen minutes late. Two women who might have been from different planets rather than mother and daughter followed her through the front door. Attorney L. Burton Hodges looked like the proverbial million bucks. Her suit was a designer model, and her leather pumps were not purchased at out local shopping mall. Her hair had the kind of casual, tousled look that only an expensive hairdresser could achieve. She reached out to shake my hand when Evelyn introduced us, and I was suddenly very aware of my faded jeans and baggy sweatshirt.

Glenna, on the other hand, was a leftover flower child. If not exactly pretty, she was appealing in the same ethereal way that Daisy was. There was something canned about her appearance, as though she had dressed for a costume party but gone just a bit over the top. There was too much of everything—hair, bracelets, rings. Even her greeting was too much.

"Oh, my God, I am so happy to meet you. I mean, I've heard all this great stuff. Like you must be a saint or something, taking in a kid like Daisy. The energy in this house is just so great. I could feel it as soon as I walked in the door. Do you do feng shui? The peace is just so total."

I had to laugh. "I'm afraid I can barely manage reasonably

neat most days. But I'll take the compliment anyway. Please, come in and sit down. I'll call Daisy. She'll be so happy to see you."

The other kids were back in school after the holiday break, but I didn't have Daisy enrolled yet. I was glad she would be able to see her mom and grandmother without the interruptions I could always expect when everybody was home. No matter how firmly I laid down the law about how I expected the children to behave when I had company, they could never resist the opportunity to grab attention from an adult, no matter how bad the timing. Priscilla could be counted on to whine for something she knew I wouldn't want her to have, and Jazzy nearly always threw a tantrum when she found my attention elsewhere.

Daisy came down as soon as I called her. I had done my best to spiff her up for the occasion. She was nicely dressed and her nose was wiped. There wasn't much I could do with her hair, but at least it was clean. It had taken a couple of days for Daisy's psychiatrist to get back to me, and by that time it was pretty clear that Daisy could function without medication. She was allowed to continue that way. While I couldn't be sure that was the whole reason, Daisy looked less spacey than she had when she arrived. Her speech was still pretty limited, but generally she managed to get her point across. Altogether, I was pretty pleased with the way she looked. I think I held some hope that Glenna would see Daisy differently and consider taking her only child home. I had been hard-pressed from the beginning to figure out exactly what the problem with caring for Daisy was. She took some effort, especially around meals, but I had rarely seen a child as anxious to please as this one. I found it nearly impossible to imagine dear little Daisy as oppositional or aggressive. She had developed the habit of standing next to me while I washed the dishes and just leaning into my side until I reached down for a quick hug. I hated to see Daisy go, but I just couldn't come up with a reason for her to be in foster care.

When I called her down, Daisy hopped into the living room and stopped dead in the doorway. She looked from her mother to her grandmother, not speaking and not moving. I could have kicked myself for not preparing Daisy for this visit. I thought it would be a nice surprise for her, but I couldn't have been more wrong. Daisy looked stricken. Glenna finally broke the silence.

"Daisy! Baby! I've missed you. Come give Mommy a hug."

Glenna recited this speech as though she had practiced it in front of a mirror for a long time in order to get the inflection just right.

I wasn't sure how Glenna expected Daisy to hug her, since she didn't bother to get up from the sofa. The grandmother spoke up before Daisy had a chance to respond.

"Daisy! My dear, how nice to see you. I hope you're behaving yourself."

It was Evelyn who finally walked over to Daisy and scooped her up in a big hug.

"Hey, kiddo! I'm so glad to see you. Kathy tells me you're doing just great! Look who I brought with me. You didn't expect to see Mommy today, did you?"

Daisy seemed to thaw out ever so slightly. She scooted over to hug Glenna and smiled up at her.

"Hi, Mommy. You comin to get me? I goin home?"

The words weren't clear, but Daisy's face said it all. In spite of the smile, it was tight with worry.

"Not yet, baby. Mommy still needs some help figuring things out. I think it's best if you stay here a while longer."

Mrs. Hodges made no move to get up. She sat very erect with her hands folded stiffly in her lap. Daisy looked from her mother to grandmother as though waiting for some clue about what was expected of her. After an interminable period, and with a small push from Glenna, Daisy scampered over to her grandmother. Daisy's nose was beginning to drip again and she swiped at it with the palm of her hand before giving Mrs. Hodges a hug. A visible shudder passed over her and she moved to hold her small granddaughter at arm's length.

"Really, Daisy. You must learn to use a handkerchief." The note of disgust in Mrs. Hodges's voice was unmistakable.

I gave Daisy a small hug and handed her a tissue before going to the kitchen to prepare tea for everyone. Evelyn offered to help me, but I was fairly certain she was just looking for an excuse to escape from the odd scene in the living room.

"I feel like I'm watching a car wreck," she whispered to me while I got out the teacups. "I don't want to watch, but I can't look away."

I knew how she felt. This was the strangest reunion I had ever witnessed, and I had been privy to some odd ones. Even the awkwardness of meeting in the home of a stranger couldn't account for the stiffness of these people with one another.

"What type of law do you practice, Mrs. Hodges?" I asked when we settled down with our tea.

"I'm retired, but I did practice general law. Estate planning, that sort of thing. Very dry, I'm afraid. I give my time to the church now. It is far more rewarding. Are you and Mr. Harrison Catholic?"

"No," I answered with a smile, "our families have been Protestant for generations. We have the occasional Mormon thrown in for variety and even a Quaker or two. Is Daisy used to going to mass?"

Glenna shot a look in her mother's direction.

"I don't get my mother's deal with organized religion. The universe is my religion. Know what I mean? She takes Daisy to church sometimes, but I don't buy that stuff. I mean, I don't care if Daisy goes, but I talk to her about what I believe, too."

"I'm sure Mrs. Harrison doesn't need to hear about the nonsense that passes for theology to an untrained mind, Glenna," Mrs. Hodges responded coldly.

As the tension built up between the two women in her life, Daisy shrank down into the sofa cushions. She began a pattern I was beginning to recognize, rocking rapidly back and forth, flapping her hands, and chanting from one to ten, over and over, all in a futile effort to wrest some control from her chaotic world.

I found myself uncomfortably perched on the horns of a familiar dilemma. Neither Glenna nor Mrs. Hodges seemed at all inclined to consider Daisy's feelings in what I felt quite sure was a continuing battle of wills. So there I sat, wanting to comfort a little girl I could not claim as mine. She needed someone to hang on to just then, and her family didn't appear to be up to the task. But I knew that my stepping in could permanently damage any relationship I hoped to form with her mother, a relationship that Daisy needed us to have if we were going to work together to help this needy little girl.

Evelyn didn't seem to share my reservations. Her voice was curt as she wasted no time intervening.

"That's grown-up talk, ladies. This time is for Daisy. Why don't you have Kathy and Daisy show you her room, Glenna? Mrs. Hodges, may I get you some more tea?"

It was a blatant ploy to separate the two and it worked. Away from her mother, Glenna was able to muster some interest in her daughter. Not much, but enough to ask if she had what she needed for school and to find out about the girls who shared her living space. Her eyes widened when she saw four beds in Daisy's room.

"Daisy's used to having her own space. I'm not sure she should be sharing with other kids. Is there any way that could happen?"

I kept my voice even when I answered.

"I'm afraid not, Glenna. Kids lose a lot when they come into foster care. Not just their families but their houses and schools and pets and friends. They have to get used to a lot of changes in a big hurry. It's hard on kids, but most of them adapt to the physical changes pretty quickly. It's the people they miss. Not the stuff. Daisy is doing just fine with the other girls."

Any implied criticism was lost on Glenna. She was already

wandering off to explore the rest of the upstairs. I pulled the door to the room Angie and Neddy shared firmly shut before Glenna could walk in.

Glenna was spared a lecture about my children's right to privacy by the ringing of the telephone. It was home-finding, asking if I could help them out with a seven-year-old for a few days. Normally, caring for an extra little girl wouldn't have required much from me, but my home-finder, Susan, rather sheepishly told me it was the child's birthday. I would have to come up with some sort of celebration for a kid who didn't have much to celebrate.

In spite of the disruption, I was delighted to have a valid excuse for winding up Daisy's visit. Not that I found her family scary or intimidating. Even Glenna's problem with boundaries was less rude than it was childish. I probably would have found Mrs. Hodges pretty interesting under other circumstances. They just irritated me on some gut level that had to do with their inability to talk to Daisy. Emotionally, this little girl had been hit by a truck, and the best her mother or grandmother could come up with was to ask about her behavior and to worry about her accommodations. I wanted them to hold her, to be gentle with her, to really want to know how she was holding up.

But that was not going to happen, at least not that day. While the three women gathered coats and purses, Daisy fell apart. It wasn't a gradual fall. It was a dramatic crash. Her flapping and spinning escalated until she was nearly bouncing off the walls. She seemed frantic to get Glenna's attention, pulling on her handbag, climbing across the kitchen chairs, and yapping like a small puppy. For the first time since her arrival, I saw the hyper-activity and bizarre behavior that had been reported. The wilder Daisy got, the more anxious Glenna became. She didn't tell Daisy to settle down as much as plead with her to do so. The hesitancy and uncertainty in her voice was not lost on Daisy, who responded with a maniacal laugh and dash toward her mother. With her mother, grandmother, and social worker all standing there, I was reluctant to intervene, and I might not have had Daisy not begun pounding on Glenna's back. The blows could not have hurt much. It would have been like being beaten by a butterfly, but it needed to stop. I caught Daisy from behind, wrapping my arms around her thin frame and dropping to the floor. Held as she was, Daisy had no choice but to flop down with me. There she sat, her breath coming in quick, shallow gulps.

"Daisy," I said firmly, "you need to stop. Can you do that by yourself, or do you need me to help you?"

Daisy looked up at me with panicked eyes. "Help." The word was spoken so softly I had to lean in to catch it.

"All right. I want you to take some deep breaths like I showed you. When you calm down, I want you to go upstairs and get the clay out of the art box. I want you to sit at the table in the den and play with it until I come up. Can you do that?"

After a moment, Daisy nodded. She sat for a minute, maybe two, breathing heavily. I relaxed my grip and helped her up. She didn't attempt to speak to her mother or grandmother but did as I asked and plodded upstairs with the heavy tread of the defeated. I heard the sound of the closet in the den being opened and closed, then quiet.

I turned to find Evelyn slightly bug-eyed, but neither Glenna nor Mrs. Hodges acted as though anything was amiss. They certainly gave no outward sign that they had just been through a pretty remarkable meltdown. I felt a bit like Alice at the mad tea party where everyone was crazy but me. Mrs. Hodges put on her coat while Glenna fished through her bag for a stick of chewing gum. Evelyn finally broke the silence.

"Is, uh, that pretty typical behavior for Daisy?" she asked uncertainly.

"Pretty much," Glenna responded. "Sometimes it's a lot worse. You can see why I can't take care of her. She just gets out of control, and I don't know what to do with her. I thought the hospital would help, but they seemed to think everything was my fault. Like making me take a parenting class is going to change Daisy."

An uncomfortable silence followed, then the talk turned not to therapy or how we might work together to help Daisy get through the trauma of possible sexual abuse, but rather to her educational plan. Mrs. Hodges brought it up.

"Daisy is a bit limited. But I suppose you've noticed that. We don't expect miracles, but we hope that with help she can remain in a regular classroom. I have arranged for her previous school to transfer her records. I assume your school will be able to provide her with the same services."

I didn't plan on getting into a confrontation with Mrs.

Hodges over her granddaughter's intelligence, but I wasn't at all sure that Daisy was as limited as she appeared. I certainly wasn't about to write off a six-year-old as a special needs child without a lot more information. Before any judgment was made about her native intelligence, she at least deserved some time in a stable home, without the dulling effects of a bag full of medications and without the daily trauma of being abused by her mother's boyfriend.

The good-byes were perfunctory, with no one sure how to make a graceful exit.

I went up to check on Daisy. She had taken the clay out, but it lay unopened on the table. Daisy had wrapped herself in a faded old quilt and was lying on the sofa in the den, not sleeping but close to it, thumb in her mouth and eyelids heavy. I didn't want her to sleep. It felt too much like escape. I hoped she might talk to me about the visit and what had happened at the end. But talk seemed beyond her just now. Still, I gently unwrapped the quilt and pulled Daisy upright, holding her close for a minute before guiding her downstairs.

With my house my own again, I made myself a fresh cup of tea and set about picking up the kitchen so I could get a cake in the oven and start lunch for the little girls. Daisy trailed my every move, walking so close to my heels that I tripped over her every time I turned around.

"Hey, Daisy," I said the third time I bumped into her, "let's find something for you to do. Do you like puzzles?"

Daisy's face lit up, and she began to spin and flap her arms. "Yah! I like. I like puzzles. I do. Okay?"

Daisy's enthusiasm about so small a thing as a puzzle made me smile, and I was nearly able to forget her behavior of only an hour before. She was like a neglected puppy who had finally met a friendly soul. Her gratitude was touching in a sad kind of way.

I found the pile of puzzles in the toy cabinet. As usual, they were all mixed together. I tried to keep the preschool puzzles separate from the jigsaw puzzles that the older kids used, but it was a losing battle. I had long since learned to be satisfied with getting all the pieces back in the right boxes. I put an eight-inch stack of puzzles in the middle of the kitchen table.

"Some of these are kind of hard, sweetie. Here. How about this one? I'll bet you can put this together."

I picked out a simple eight-piece inset puzzle and set it in front of Daisy. Since it would have been easy for a much younger child, I was sure Daisy could manage it. I wanted to be sure to start her off with something that guaranteed success. I left Daisy with the puzzles and returned to the sink. The sun had faded and the snow that had been predicted earlier was finally starting to sputter to the ground. Already, the roads looked slick. I was halfheartedly washing dishes and letting my mind wander. Karen and Jazzy were due home from preschool in about an hour. I hoped the snow wouldn't pick up until after that. I hated having my little ones out on our isolated back roads in bad weather. In the still of the morning, it was easy to let one task follow another. Before long, I had wiped down the refrigerator and folded a load of clothes. The cake went into the oven. I put a pot of leftover soup on the stove to simmer. I heard a small whimper and realized that Daisy had noticed the soup and was worried about having to eat it, soup being one of the many things she couldn't abide swallowing.

"It's all right, honey. I'm not going to make you eat the soup."

I approached the table where Daisy was sitting and stopped short. The puzzles were done. Not just the easy ones but the hard ones, too. The ones that the older kids struggled with. Even the two-hundred-piece Noah's Ark puzzle that only Priscilla was able to complete was finished and pushed to the center of the table.

"Looks like we'll have to get some harder puzzles for you, Daisy," I said with as much nonchalance as I could muster.

Daisy smiled her sweet little out-to-lunch smile and slowly took apart a one-hundred-piece puzzle and placed each piece meticulously upside down in front of her. Then, with only occasional hesitation, she put it back together with no picture to guide her. It would have been quite a feat for any child, but for spacey Daisy it was nothing short of miraculous. When she finished, we sat and grinned at each other like two little kids sharing a birthday secret.

Moments like these are rare for me. Having so many children makes it hard to come up with the special alone times that all of the kids need from time to time. All too soon, Karen and Jazzy tumbled in the door, snow-covered and wanting lunch. I wanted to sit with Daisy for just a few more minutes. I wanted to find a moment to call her social worker and tell her just what I thought about Daisy's so-called limitations. But Jazzy had fallen on the way in the door and needed me to kiss her bumped knee, and

Karen had to tell me just how disgusting Bobby was on the bus. So I ladled soup and listened to stories, and my moment with Daisy passed. I finished picking up the table after lunch. I put the dishes in the sink and wiped up some spilled milk, but I left the upside-down puzzle on the table for the rest of the afternoon as proof that I wasn't crazy, that Daisy had really done it.

The little girl we were expecting arrived in the late afternoon. Robin, a pale slip of a girl, and her sister had been removed from their foster home because of some suspicion of abuse. I didn't know the family and I didn't have any details, but the child was clean and well dressed. More important, she was distraught, both at being removed and at being separated from her sister.

"I don't know why they took us," she wailed over and over. "It was the best place I ever been. Mama Corrine loves us. I want to go home."

I felt terrible for Robin. It was a heck of a thing to happen to her on her birthday.

I had no time to shop for gifts, but I keep a stash of generic presents in my closet for just this kind of emergency. I had a Slinky, some coloring books, and art supplies, but I didn't have anything special. I called Bruce at work, and he agreed to stop at the mall and scout the toy store for something to take at least some of the sting out of a truly awful day. Angie offered to decorate the cake when she got home. She has a flair for this sort of thing anyway, and because she felt so sorry for Robin, she really outdid herself. It was a marvel of pink flowers on a purple background and had Robin's name piped in white across the top.

We kept the whole thing hush-hush until after dinner. The

little girls took Robin upstairs to play while Neddy and I set the table with Barbie plates and cups. Ben lit the candles, and carefully arranged the rather extraordinary pile of beautifully wrapped presents Bruce had brought home. Angie led Robin to the kitchen and we greeted her with a chorus of "Happy Birthday," sung with off-key gusto. Robin was speechless.

She blew out the candles and attacked the gifts, exclaiming over the Barbie doll, the games, and the jewelry kit. We were well into seconds on cake and ice cream when Robin finally asked, "Do you do this for all your foster kids?"

"Just the ones lucky enough to have their eighth birthday on the day they arrive," Bruce answered.

"Uh, it's not my birthday." Robin looked pained.

"It's not," I said flatly.

"It's my sister's birthday. She's eleven. We were supposed to have a party for her, but then we got tooken." Robin was quiet for a second. "Do I have to give the stuff back?"

Of course we let Robin keep the gifts. She had already had a tough day, and I wasn't going to make it worse by taking her new doll away. That night Bruce and I had a good laugh about the whole mix-up, but we were sorry to think that somewhere out there was a little girl having a miserable birthday.

Four

Each child comes to me with a set of special needs based just on the fact that she has landed on the doorstep of a stranger. Add to that the different physical, emotional, social, and educational issues, and you come up with a lot of work to do. The sheer number of kids, coupled with the variety of problems they present, would overwhelm me if I didn't make some attempt to prioritize what I need to do. Sometimes this meant that the more competent kids, or at least the less noisy and less obviously disturbed ones, got short shift. I wished it was different. Most of us who end up doing social service work are fixers and healers by nature. But in the real world, even Superwoman can't do everything, and I am anything but Superwoman. My heroine on more days than I care to admit to would have been Mediocre Woman, Mistress of Getting at Least Something Accomplished.

The "to do" list for Daisy was so long that it was hard to know where to start. There were the phobias. Daisy was afraid of everything: Storms, bugs, water, the dark, dogs, and bridges were just a few of the things I found that reduced her to a quivering heap. Educationally, she was dismal in some areas and looked nearly gifted in others. An appointment to have tubes placed in her ears had already been scheduled by the time I met her. That meant having to deal with her fear of doctors, but that minor bit of surgery did cause a noticeable improvement in her speech almost right away. A secondary benefit was that the green sludge in her nose finally dried up. I wanted Daisy assessed by someone who could talk to me about her flapping and spinning, behaviors that looked almost autistic, although she was clearly too connected and engaged for that to be a diagnosis. She needed to see a dentist, but considering her behavior with the ear doctor, I decided to put that appointment on hold. At least Daisy was hooked up with an excellent therapist. Toni Tonelli worked at the Children's Clinic with Andrew Donovan. She was wonderful about giving me direction in handling some of Daisy's more troubling behaviors. More important, she was always available to talk with me. Not all therapists understand the reality of fostering. The therapist sees the child for an hour a week. The rest of the time, I'm on. If I'm not guided and supported, it's the child who suffers.

Not eating affected so many parts of Daisy's day that I decided to tackle that problem right away. It was a tricky one that I rarely came up against; more often, the kids who came to me had a history of deprivation. They tended to eat everything in sight. Daisy was one of only a handful who seemed not just fussy or used to cheese puffs for breakfast but truly nauseated by the prospect of consuming food. That made me wonder whether there might be some sensory integration problems. Tags on her clothes bothered her, as did the seams in her socks. She would spin in a circle until somebody stopped her, she was chronically disorganized, and she could never locate her backpack or sneakers. I was just beginning to read about this condition, whereby a difficulty in processing information is then relieved through the senses. This definition of the disorder fit Daisy to a T, and so, in the absence of any other explanation, I decided to approach the problem from that angle.

Several times a day, I sat with Daisy at the table. I would bring out something bland, like apple juice or vanilla yogurt. We would start with a drop on her tongue, increasing the amount slowly until she was able to swallow a teaspoon of it without gagging. At the same time I would brush her arm or stroke her back. I hoped to connect those sensations that Daisy enjoyed with the experience of eating. Daisy was fairly compliant with this regimen. At least she never outright refused, although, goodness knows, she cried and moaned as though I expected her to consume a live cockroach rather than a small spoonful of mashed potato. We never did the work when there was a real meal on the table. I wanted to remove the anxiety of the dinner hour. The food was there; she could eat it or not. Progress was slow but noticeable. Fruit was adapted to pretty quickly. She added rice and the occasional vegetable to her menu. As the variety of food increased, along with the volume of food she consumed, Daisy began to put on some much-needed weight. A pound the first month, then another and another. When adults add five or six pounds to their frames, it's unlikely that anyone will notice, but when a thirty-six-pound kid adds that much, it really shows.

One surprise was that although she was very proud of her new abilities, she didn't carry them over to visits home.

Because this was a voluntary placement, Glenna could see Daisy whenever she liked. Mrs. Hodges was willing to do a lot of the driving and I was able to combine some trips to do the rest. As a result, Daisy was spending at least a few hours every Saturday with her mother. At those weekly visits, she remained as oppositional as ever.

It was hard for me to believe that the gentle little girl I knew could be the same Daisy who kicked her mother and dumped a full box of cereal down the heating duct on one particular Saturday. I heard the story from Mrs. Hodges when she brought Daisy back.

"Glenna has no idea how to discipline that child," she reported angrily. "How could she? She's still a child herself. All this nonsense about karma and palm reading."

Mrs. Hodges hands were clasped firmly around the handle of her bag, and her voice shook. "The scene I walked in on! Daisy was completely out of control, and so was Glenna. I tried to speak to her about catechism for the child and she wouldn't even discuss it."

I had to agree with Glenna about that.

Nevertheless, at home with us, Daisy was making some good progress, and I was feeling good about what was happening. Good feelings I needed, because not everything else at home was going smoothly.

Jazzy was wearing me down, inch by screaming inch. All of the gains she had made over the late fall and early winter had disappeared until, as February waned, I began to doubt that they had ever existed anywhere but in my imagination. Everyone noticed it. Not just our family but her teachers and her therapist, Andrew, commented on how much more fragile she was, how quick to rage and difficult to soothe.

Like all of my children, Jazzy needed a foster mother with lots of time for her. There were some lost years to make up for. What she got was me, often scattered, always overbooked, and seldom certain about what I was doing. I was used to operating in a low-grade crisis mode. I also found myself giving in to Jazzy's increasingly unreasonable demands in order to avoid a confrontation.

Naturally, Jazzy had figured that out long before I did. As any child would, she made good use of the power. It wasn't until her early March visit with her adoption worker that I realized that things had to change and change quickly, not for my sake but for Jazzy's.

I had remarkably good luck, first with Jazzy's ongoing worker and then with her adoption worker. Lauren Hightower had a lot of adoption experience behind her. I knew she was good when she took several weeks getting to know Jazzy before she started to think about an appropriate adoptive match for her. She spent time with Jazzy at our house before taking her out alone for walks and car rides so that she would have a real sense of just who this child was. I was used to having Lauren stop by several times a month, but this time the visit felt different. For one thing, she set up a time when she knew Jazzy would be in school.

I could guess what was coming. One might have expected that finding a family wanting to adopt a kid who had actually torn curtains from their rods while in a rage might be difficult, but that wasn't the case. In truth, every kid who lands on the adoption track in social services has special needs. These kids are rarely the healthy, bright, legally free infants that a lot of people think of when you mention adoption. The children I know are older. They have brothers and sisters. They often have medical problems and difficulty in school. They have a history of loss and trauma and abuse that leaves wounds not easily healed. Most troubling for many families is that many of these children are still in the legal process of being freed for adoption. These kids are referred to as legal-risk kids. What that means is that children are placed in the families hoping to adopt them before the case is heard in court. The outcome of any case is uncertain. A judge might well deem that the evidence for terminating parental rights is not strong enough and send a child home. It doesn't happen often, but it does happen. It is only fair to let a family know before they take a child that the situation is not clear-cut.

Jazzy was only three. She was bright and healthy and attractive. Her parents had not accepted any services and had shown up in court so drunk that they were arrested on the spot. Dad had recently been arrested again on assault charges. It was unlikely that any judge would send Jazzy back to them. Given the problems a lot of our kids had, a temper tantrum seemed not such a bad thing.

Lauren came by on one of those brilliant not-quite-spring days when all good things seem possible. She was a pretty woman with an open face framed by soft curls. Usually she was smiling, but that day she looked solemn. We made small talk for a few minutes before she came to the point of her visit.

"So. Do you want the good news or the bad news?"

"Let's start with the bad news. At least I'll have something to look forward to."

"Okay. The bad news is I have a family for Jazzy."

Knowing it was coming didn't make it any easier to hear. There were many times during the day when Jazzy drove me to the brink of crazy. Times when I wasn't sure I had another day of caring for her in me. She was aggravating and demanding and hard, hard, hard, but I had held her when she cried. I had listened to her when she told of being locked in a closet and thrown against walls. She had trusted me when she had no reason to trust anybody. Her screams were a testament to that trust. I had nursed her through ear infections and missed parental visits. I helped her build her first snowman. I took pictures of her as an angel in our Christmas pageant. I didn't always think I could live with her. Now I had to figure out how to live without her.

I took a sip of cold coffee and swallowed before I could speak. "What's the good news?"

Lauren smiled. "The good news is that I have a family for Jazzy. Are you ready to hear about them?"

"I guess."

"They're perfect. Mid-thirties with no children but an extended family that's around a lot. Mom is a computer wizard of some sort. She works from home. Dad has his own landscaping business. They have a lovely home in a great neighborhood with a ton of kids. They're both athletes. They swim and ski and run half-marathons. They want only one child, and they really want a girl. I like them a lot. I think you will, too."

"What did they say about the tantrums?"

"You know, they really seemed to get it. They know it won't be personal. They see tantrums as a phase she has to go through before she's ready to heal and move on with her life. I like their attitude about her birth parents, too. They're angry, of course. I don't think you could hear about what her parents did to Jazzy without that. But they could understand that the parents' histories are probably similar to Jazzy's, and they're just glad to have a chance to make sure that her life will be different."

Lauren's voice was quiet, almost hypnotic. As she continued to talk about the family, I guess I took some of it in, but mostly I was processing the only important thought. My Jazzy had a family. She was leaving. I was just her for-a-while Mom. Not the real thing. Temporary. Fake. No wonder kids hate foster care.

Lauren stayed until Jazzy and Karen came home. I think she

timed things so that if I had a hard time, I would have a chance to collect myself before I saw Jazzy. She wasn't staying to tell Jazzy about her family. Because Jazzy was so young, Lauren had decided to do a blind meeting before that. She would take Jazzy to some kid-friendly place and introduce the Hamiltons in a casual way. Then, when the conversation took place, Jazzy would have faces to put with the information.

I had some reservations about the blind meeting idea, although it is a pretty common practice. I always feel as if the kid is there for inspection. If she acts up or is unattractive, a family could back out without the child having to know about it. That had happened a few times. A family met a child and decided that the match was just not good. While I could understand a family's reluctance to make a lifetime commitment to a kid they weren't sure they could love, it feels a lot like shopping for a kid. You don't get to choose who pops out of your womb, and I'm not sure how much control you should have when you decide to adopt, because most control is only illusion. My concern is this: A family decides to adopt a little boy who looks perfect. He's bright and handsome and has a terrific sense of humor. What happens if the child becomes ill? What if there is an accident or a genetic problem that doesn't show up for a few years, and he is no longer cute or smart? Does this give a family license to say, "Hey! This isn't what I signed up for"? The way I see it, once they're yours, they're yours. They're yours when they're valedictorians, and they're yours when they're delinquents. You may be cheering when they score the winning soccer goal, or you may be giving stickers for a day with no call from the principal. You're there for your kid—no matter what—because that's what parents do.

Karen and Jazzy had gotten into a four-year-old's version of a snowball fight on the way in from the school bus, and they collapsed in the front door in a giggling heap. Watching them, I felt a dull, heavy lump rise in my throat. Everyone would miss Jazzy. For my oldest kids, her loss would land on the periphery of their busy lives. Bruce and I would grieve as we always grieved when a child we had grown to love left, but our grief would be tempered by the joy of watching the birth of a new family. Priscilla and Crystal would absorb this loss into the great chasm of all of their own losses; most of their grief would be for themselves. For Karen, it would be very different. When you're four, eighteen months is a big chunk of your life. It was time that transformed the girls from roommates to sisters.

Every time Karen rolled her eyes or wiggled her nose or cleared her throat, as she did nearly all the time now, I thought about the life she had been handed when we adopted her. It was a life she had not signed up for. She had not requested a life where children came into her family in the middle of the night. Against all odds, she would grow to love them, to expect their presence. More important, she expected us to love and protect them because that's what parents do. Then they disappeared. We did our best to explain it. We used the right words and did our best to normalize a profoundly abnormal experience. But words are so often a sham. We use them to make ourselves feel better about what we do to children. I feared that anxiety might well be the reason Karen had the obsessive need to line up her shoes every night and wash her hands twenty times a day.

Lauren spent a few minutes visiting with Jazzy and then gathered her things to leave. "Are you okay?" she asked softly.

"I will be. It isn't as though we didn't know this was coming. But I was just going to ask you the same thing. You look a little preoccupied."

"You know, some days this job really stinks."

"That doesn't sound like you. I don't mean to pry, but is it something you want to talk about?"

"I'm just so frustrated. I placed a little boy with a family about ten months ago. Things went pretty well the first few months and then just slowly started to go downhill. We have a court date next month to finalize the adoption, and now the family wants to back out."

"Is the kid really difficult?"

"All things considered, he's not doing so bad. Bedtime is a challenge. He's still hoarding food, which is starting to bother them. He's had some trouble in school. Dad is a teacher, I think he's embarrassed about that. Their older son is having a hard time. The kids fight all the time, and of course they blame my little guy for that. But you know what their big complaint is? He won't call them Mom and Dad. So what do I do? Try to talk them into doing something they don't want to do, because I don't have anything else for an eleven-year-old boy, or just accept the fact that it's over and move him to a bridge home? And how am I ever going to get this kid to buy into trying again with another family, assuming I can find one? He's had a half-dozen foster homes, and every one has bailed on him. Now this. I'm going to have to be the one to tell him that these people have changed their minds. I'm just sick about it."

"Do you ever wonder if you're always doing kids a favor by pulling them from their birth families when we have so little to offer them?"

"Not really. The first time this kid came into care he was two and had cigarette burns on his bottom. He went home the next year and was back in care at five with a broken arm. He went to an aunt that time until we found out that she's leaving him locked in her car while she's out barhopping. What else is social services supposed to do? Wait until he's dead?"

"So the answer is to get them out early and on to the adoption track while they're still young and emotionally pretty healthy," I interrupted.

"That's what the Adoption and Safe Families Act is supposed to do. But then you run the risk of destroying a family that might be saved with some extra time and services. And getting kids early is no guarantee that there won't be big problems down the road. A lot of adoptive families still come into this expecting Pollyanna. They think they'll experience instant attachment and gratitude. That just isn't going to be the case for most of our kids. They come with a heavy load of history and they aren't going to change overnight. When you get right down to it," Lauren remarked with a wry smile, "the whole social service thing is a crapshoot for kids."

That conversation stuck with me for the next few days. I had to get Jazzy ready for a move to this family. Every time she started to howl over some minor thing, I wondered if there were some other thing I could be doing, some magic trick that might help. I knew that Jazzy did not have the ability to handle a failed adoption, and I also knew that listening to a kid scream for an hour because you bought her the wrong shampoo is not everybody's idea of a good time.

The meeting with the Hamiltons was set for Saturday. When people talk about uncaring social workers, I think about the ones like Lauren, who give up a day off because it works for one of her kids.

Since Angie and Neddy were home, I put them in charge of getting Jazzy ready. Both of my older girls have a flair for hair and fashion that I am rather pitifully lacking. They kept Jazzy upstairs for nearly an hour, but the results were pretty spectacular. Jazzy was so hard to please and resistant to letting me do anything to her hair that I generally settled for pulling her long curls up into a ponytail and letting her pick out her own clothes. Granted, this led to some pretty interesting outfits, but it avoided a morning meltdown. That was all I cared about with fifteen minutes left before the bus arrived.

For the teenagers, Jazzy was the soul of cooperation. She twirled into the kitchen with a "Ta da, Mama. Ain't I just the cutest thing?" The "Mama" pained me, but I had to admit that indeed she was the cutest thing.

The girls had plaited her curls into double French braids and topped each with a crisp purple bow. Jazzy was wearing a long dress, vest, and leggings, all in different purple prints. If I had tried to pull it off, she would have looked like an upended laundry basket, but with my fashion queens overseeing the wardrobe, Jazzy looked like a small brown Annie Hall.

By the time I heard Lauren's car pull into the driveway, my stomach was churning. Lauren and Jazzy were headed for an afternoon story hour at a local library. The Hamiltons would be there at the same time, blending in with the other parents and having their first look at their new daughter. Story hour would be followed by juice and cookies. Lauren would introduce Al and Barbara Hamilton as friends of hers.

The other girls were pretty predictable in their reaction to Jazzy spending a Saturday afternoon doing something special with Lauren. Karen was nonchalant. She was going through what I hoped was a stage of not wanting to be more than a few feet away from me. As long as I wasn't going anywhere, she didn't much care if Jazzy was. Although Crystal was stoic, her bottom lip trembled when she saw me pick up Jazzy's coat. It was likely that Patty, who was already an hour late for her Saturday visit, wouldn't show at all. Even though Crystal never complained about Patty and made up excuses such as probable car trouble or confusion about times, I knew how hurt she was by her mother's lack of interest. As for Priscilla, she was fuming.

"It's not fair. If Jazzy gets to go someplace, then you have to do something special for us."

I was saved from having to respond by Daisy. "I sank we shu be gla fo her. We fwends. Wite?" Her voice was so soft and her articulation so poor that it took a minute to figure out what Daisy was saying.

"Yes, sweetie, we should be glad for her." I held Daisy's thin face between my palms. "Did anyone ever tell you that you are a very nice little person?"

Daisy smiled up at me. "No. They tell me I a bitch."

Maybe the word "bitch" triggered something for Jazzy. Maybe she sensed something was up besides a story hour. Maybe she had held herself together as long as she could. Or maybe Jazzy was just being Jazzy. Who knows? But she began to crumble with Lauren's knock on the door. Her eyes narrowed when she saw her coat in my hand.

"I don't wanna coat."

"Come on, Jazz. Lauren's here. If you want to go to story hour, you have to wear a coat."

"I don't wanna coat." Jazzy's voice took on a familiar frantic edge and the volume began to rise.

"Let's get going, hon." Lauren had walked in and was trying to diffuse the tension. She took Jazzy's arm and attempted to slip it into the sleeve of her coat while she spoke.

"No! No! No! No coat!" Now Jazzy was really screaming. She yanked her arm back and plopped on the floor, grabbing for her shoes.

"I don't want these shoes. They stupid and ugly!" Stupid and ugly was Jazzy's favorite description for anything she didn't like. Usually, that was me.

"No! No! No shoes! No coat!"

"You have to wear shoes, Jazz. It's forty degrees outside. Your feet will freeze off." Lauren was trying to reason with a kid who was past reasoning.

I had been thinking about these tantrums all week, and I had an idea. While I sure wished I had had a chance to try it out without a social worker for an audience, I was going for it anyway.

"Okay, Jazz. You don't have to wear your coat or your shoes." I sat down next to Jazz and, none too gently, pulled off her shoes.

"Come on, kiddo. Time to go."

Lauren must have thought I had lost my mind.

"Uh, Kathy? It really is cold outside. Are you sure . . . ?" Her voice trailed off.

"Jazzy's tough. Aren't you, Jazzy? She doesn't mind cold feet. Now you have fun."

Jazz just stared at me, her mouth agape. She stood up slowly and walked toward the door, shooting glances over her shoulder at me to make sure I knew she was really heading out coatless and in her stocking feet.

"Wait a minute, Peanut. You can't go out in your stocking feet."

Jazz looked vastly relieved until I bent down and took off her tights and stuffed them into my pocket.

"We don't want them to get dirty, do we?"

Poor Jazz was in a pickle now. She didn't really want to go out half-dressed. She just wanted a power struggle, which I wasn't giving her.

Lauren reluctantly took Jazz by the hand. "Well, I guess we'll see you later."

"All right. Have fun."

"Mommy! You let Jazzy go out in her bare feets," cried Karen as the door closed.

"I guess I did, didn't I?" I was considerably less confident now that Jazz was actually out the door. It was just sinking in that I had sent a four-year-old out to meet her new family, coatless and shoeless in temperatures barely above freezing.

"That's not fair," Priscilla whined. "You always make me wear shoes. How come Jazzy always gets her own way?"

"For crying out loud, Priscilla. Will you give it a rest? Freezing your feet off is not some privilege I've been keeping from you."

Daisy was rocking back and forth and choking back sobs.

"Will her feets fall off? Will her die?"

Crystal rolled her eyes. "You don't die from cold feet. Besides, I don't think Kathy thought she would really go out like that. Did you, Kathy?"

At that moment I'm not sure what I thought, beyond knowing that I had to do something about Jazzy's tantrums before we began to transition her to the Hamiltons. Unfortunately, I hadn't figured out what to do if she called my bluff.

There was a soft knock at the door. I let out a long sigh of relief and tried to sound casual when I opened it.

"That was quick."

Lauren guided Jazzy inside.

"I think Jazz has something to tell you."

Jazz looked up at me with huge, tear-filled eyes.

"What is it, Jazz?"

"My feets are cold," she finally blurted out between an-guished sobs.

It would have taken a much harder heart than mine to make her suffer any longer.

"Well, I bet they are." I gathered Jazz up in a bear hug. "Let's warm them up and get your tights and shoes on."

I rubbed her red little feet between my hands and blew on them until she stopped crying and let me dress her. I didn't ask her about her coat. I just held it out and she put it on without comment. Properly dressed, she left without a word or a back-ward glance, embarrassed I suppose at what must have felt like a loss of face in front of Lauren and the girls.

My afternoon was far more quiet than I was used to. Not only was Jazz gone, but Patty finally showed up to get Crystal, a full two hours late and chock-full of excuses about lost keys and heavy traffic. I was sorely tempted to tell her that it was too late for Crystal to go out now, but as much as I would have liked to punish Patty, there was no way I could hurt Crystal.

"You have to have her back by six, Patty. We have church in the morning, and Crystal is supposed to go early to help set up for Sunday school."

"That doesn't give us much time," Patty whined, sounding an awful lot like Priscilla.

"I know. Maybe next week you can be here on time."

I was thoroughly annoyed as I watched Crystal leave, and it was, of all silly things, because of her coat. In the late fall, I had ordered each of the girls their outerwear from a mail-order com-pany. Although the prices are high, the quality is excellent. We have a cold climate, and my girls spend a lot of time outside. When the weather turns cold, Bruce sprays a spot in the field so the kids can ice-skate. When the snow flies, he uses the snow-blower to build a huge conical snow mountain. Since the girls are outdoors for hours sometimes, they need warm clothes. I don't mind spending the money for something that will get so much use.

This year I had purchased a beautiful purple and teal snow-suit for Crystal. She loved it, and she looked like a princess in it. Then, just after Christmas, Patty bought her a new coat. It was silver and black and clearly meant for a boy. Crystal wouldn't admit to hating the jacket, but it was such a dilemma for her. For days she dutifully put the jacket on and marched off to school looking glum. I couldn't tell her not to wear it. After all, it was a gift from her mother. Crystal solved the problem herself by put-ting it in the wash one morning. Wearing her purple coat for the one day seemed to break the ice for her. She never wore the sil-ver jacket again unless she was going to visit her mother. Then she wouldn't wear anything else. Compared with other prob-lems I had with Patty, the coat was a small thing, but it was a big deal for Crystal, and I let it bother me more than I should have.

Crystal would probably return from this visit as she did from every visit, with bags of tube tops, platform-heeled shoes, and miniskirts that would have been over the top for a teenager, never mind for a third-grader. It was such a problem. Unlike the coat, which was just ugly, these were inappropriate and she couldn't wear them. If Patty wanted to waste her money on things she knew Crystal shouldn't have, that was her business.

Bruce was working and my teens had left for a basketball

game. I set Daisy, Priscilla, and Karen up with Play-Doh and went upstairs to change sheets and pick up a bit. My mind hopscotched from thought to thought, kid to kid as I straightened the dollhouse furniture and retrieved a sock from under Priscilla's bed to add to the pile of sheets I had already pulled off the beds. I made Jazzy's bed first, then Crystal's. I was tucking the blankets under Daisy's mattress when my fingers hit against something hard wedged between the mattress and the box spring. I lifted the mattress slightly and pulled out a notebook. It was one of mine. I had a habit of keeping notes in journals I stashed all over the house. It was a terrible system. Since I could never find the one I was looking for without a treasure hunt, when this one had gone missing a few days earlier, I hadn't given it another thought. I really couldn't imagine what Daisy would have wanted with a journal. There was always plenty of paper in the art supplies closet, and the girls could take what they wanted.

I felt a smidgeon of guilt looking in the book. It was clearly not intended for my eyes, and even young children are entitled to some privacy. Nevertheless, given how little I actually knew about Daisy, I couldn't resist taking a peek.

The first several pages were blank. Then there were a few pages of typical children's drawings of houses and rainbows. The remaining pages were not so typical. They were crude pictures, done in black crayon, showing a stick figure of a man with a large protrusion that could only have been an erect penis. There was no doubt about that, even to my untrained eye. The figure was large, taking up fully half the page. There was another, much smaller figure in the lower left-hand corner. A third, tiny figure floated off at the top of the page.

Any doubts I might have harbored about whether Daisy had been sexually abused vanished with that picture. It wasn't the sort of thing a child would draw without some experience. The only question left was what to do with the information. I would have to share it with Evelyn and also with Daisy's therapist. Anyway, I couldn't talk to anyone until Monday. The more immediate problem I faced was what to say to Daisy. I assumed she intended to keep the journal private, or she wouldn't have hidden it so well. That might mean that she wasn't ready to talk about what had happened to her, or it might mean that she didn't know she could. I was feeling my way here, but it seemed as though I had to at least give her the opportunity to talk to me and make it clear that, no matter what she told me, I wouldn't judge her or hold her responsible. I figured I had only another half hour or so before Jazzy returned. Because I wanted to do this in relative peace, with no small amount of trepidation I called Daisy to come upstairs.

"Hey, kiddo. Could you come sit with me for a minute? I need to talk to you."

"Are you ma a me?" she asked with a worried expression.

I was having less trouble understanding Daisy, although she was still dropping the final consonants of her words.

"I'm not mad, Daisy, but I am a little worried. I was making your bed and I found the pictures you drew. Hey! You don't need to get upset," I said as Daisy bit her bottom lip and began to rock back and forth. "I'm really not mad. But sometimes kids draw pictures of things that are too hard to talk about. Is that what you did? Drew something that you wished you could tell someone about?"

Daisy moved her head in a nearly imperceptible nod.

"Do you think you could tell me about this one?"

For a long minute there was only silence, then Daisy dropped her head and sobbed quietly into her hands. It was such an adult gesture from so small a child that it broke my heart. I let her cry for several minutes while I pulled her close and rubbed her bony back.

"I do the ba thing." The words were muffled, coming from the vicinity of my armpit.

"Who did you do it with?" Let the lawyers worry about leading questions. I had to worry about Daisy.

"Wif Frank."

"Who's Frank?"

"He live with us but not now."

"Was Frank Mommy's boyfriend?"

Another nod.

"Daisy," I said, pulling her face up so I could look into her eyes. "You need to listen to me. This is important. When a grown-up does something like this with a kid, it is never the kid's fault. He may tell you it is because he doesn't want you to talk about it, but it never is. Now I have to ask you some hard questions so that I'll know what to do next. Can you tell me what the bad thing was that Frank made you do?"

Daisy made the smallest of gestures to her mouth.

"He made you put your mouth on him?"

Another nod.

"Did he touch you?"

Daisy blinked hard and swallowed before she nodded again.

"Can you show me where?"

Daisy pointed between her legs.

I hated to keep asking Daisy these questions. I felt as if I were violating her all over again, but I needed all the information I could get before I called social services to file the report.

"Can you tell me what he touched you with, honey? What part of his body?"

"The ba thing. He touched me with his ba thing."

"I have just one more question, Daisy, and then we'll be all done. Where was your mommy when Frank did these things to you?"

Daisy stared into empty space, rocking back and forth, her eyes so sad and empty that she could have been one hundred instead of six.

"I call Mommy," she whispered. "I call and call, but her never come."

Daisy and I rocked together. For how long, I really couldn't say. We didn't talk. We just held each other.

I'm a pretty pragmatic person, and, goodness knows, by this time I had seen the seamier side of life often enough that it should no longer have been such a shock to me, but when it came to sexual abuse of little children, it always was. I just can't wrap my mind around it. I get other things. I can understand how someone becomes overwhelmed and hits a kid. I can picture a life so out of control that babies are neglected and the line is crossed to abuse. I don't like it, and it certainly isn't benign, but I can make such things real to me and retain some empathy. But I can't find the place in a human soul that allows space to do such a thing to an innocent child.

Eventually, I had to come up for air. Work rescued me. There was dinner to make and other children to see to. Clothes needed washing and the beds still weren't made.

A much subdued Daisy wasn't up to joining the girls. She took a baby doll to the sofa and cuddled under a blanket, looking at picture books and talking softly to herself. I couldn't hear the words, but the tone was soft. I could catch no undertone of anger. I couldn't say as much for myself.

Five

There is a bit of emotional feast or famine about my life. Weeks, even months, can slip by marked by nothing more significant than a lost tooth or a birthday celebration. During these quiet times it is possible to forget what simmers beneath the surface. I see to the house and the laundry, the meals and the children. Friends stop by. I visit the bookstore. These are the days I use to recharge my batteries and prepare for the inevitable, the weeks and months when the pot boils over. Times when the illusion of normal shatters and everyone is in crisis. Such was the March when Karen turned five.

Daisy's disclosures of sexual abuse were the beginning. I suppose it was too much to expect that anything about it would be easy. One might have guessed that I would make a phone call to some person in authority, who would ride to the rescue on the modern-day equivalent of a white horse. But it was a lot more complicated than that. I did call Evelyn. She expressed dismay but no surprise. It was more information than had been received while Daisy was hospitalized, but not much. The problem was that although Daisy had done some pointing and nodding, she hadn't actually said a lot. Finger pointings and nods don't translate well to paper. In the cool contrast of black ink on white paper, the reality of Daisy's pain and fear were lost. When questioned by a woman from the Child Sexual Assault Unit in the district attorney's office, she hadn't offered even that much. She just sat and rocked and flapped her hands, which made her look not just crazy but none too bright. Even Daisy's therapist, Toni, had little luck with getting the kind of disclosure from her that one could take to court.

At least Glenna seemed convinced that Frank had molested Daisy. That didn't translate into Glenna asking to have Daisy returned to her. In fact, it did just the opposite. She expressed relief to have Daisy in care, where people with experience in these matters could help her.

"You have to be kidding!" I said when Evelyn passed that information on to me. "Daisy's been here for over three months, and Glenna hasn't even taken her overnight. She's doing so well. She's eating better and keeping up in school. I'm beginning to feel like a babysitter, although a babysitter would be making a lot more money. What's she waiting for? Daisy to turn eighteen?"

"Well, the home visits aren't going very well. Daisy is still a problem for Glenna. I have to admit I haven't seen a kid quite so oppositional with a parent before. When I picked her up last week, Daisy was standing in the middle of the kitchen table, screaming like a banshee because Glenna wouldn't let her eat applesauce out of the jar with her fingers. You really wouldn't believe she was the same kid you have here."

And here Daisy was, if not what one could call typical, certainly not as hard as a lot of other kids I've had. She still flapped her hands and spun a lot. Her language skills were pretty far behind, and many foods still made her gag, but Daisy was unfailingly kind and gentle to the other girls. I considered that a trait far more important than the ability to swallow a peanut butter sandwich. While my worries about Daisy were considerable, they weren't the only thing going on for me.

Transition defines life for children in care. Home to home, school to school, family to family, my children are experienced if unwilling travelers. They leave behind siblings and grandparents, friends and pets. They move on to new places, where even their underwear may really belong to someone else.

Now it was Jazzy's turn. Al and Barbara Hamilton met her at her bubbly, engaging best and were captivated. They shared juice and crackers, and when Jazzy stumbled, Al was there to pick her up. She rewarded him with a warm hug. He told me later he never wanted to let her go again.

For now, we had a lot of work to do. First, there was the disclosure meeting to get through. For two grueling hours, Lauren and I sat with the Hamiltons in a windowless room in the social service office, going over medical reports, psychiatric profiles, and family history. They heard it all—the good, the bad, and the really scary. Having been on the other side of the table at a disclosure meeting for each of my daughters, I knew that hearing and believing are two very different things when you are smitten with a child. Words like family history of mental illness, attachment disorder, and prenatal drug and alcohol abuse have a way of skimming over the surface of a brain in love. No way, I remember thinking when I heard them. Not my Neddy. Not my Angie. Not my Karen. Their lives will be different because they will have us. We can save them from all of it. The arrogance can be pretty amazing.

With the disclosure duly given and summarily dismissed, the Hamiltons were introduced to Jazz as the mom and dad who had been looking for a little girl just like her to make a family with. But while they may well have needed a little girl, Jazzy didn't see herself in need of parents. She had a set, thank you very much. She was friendly enough, if a bit distant with them when they came to visit. Why not? They came with gifts and eyes for only her, but when it came time for them to take her out, Jazz was having none of it.

"I don't want a new mommy and daddy," was how Jazzy put it when Bruce and I dropped the news that in four short weeks she would be moving and that the time had come for visiting her new house. "I got you. You my mommy and daddy."

"Actually, sweetie, Kathy and I are your for-a-while mom and dad," Bruce replied quietly. "Remember when we talked about this with Dr. Drew? Roberto and Diane are your birth parents. They love you, but they can't take care of you. They can't keep you safe. We're your foster parents. We love you, too, but you need a forever family. That's who Al and Barbara are. They'll be the family who will always love you and take care of you. Their home is the place where you will grow up."

"How come Karen grows up here? How come you keep her and not me?"

I thought it best to give Jazz not information but words for what she must be feeling.

"I'll bet that makes you pretty angry."

"I won't give you any more kisses ever," she said, with her little lip quivering.

"I don't blame you, Jazz. I'd be pretty mad, too. But I can promise you something. You won't always feel so angry. Someday it's going to feel as if Al and Barbara have always been your mom and dad. You'll still remember us and I know we'll always remember you, but it won't feel bad. It will be a nice remembering."

If the Hamiltons were put off by Jazz's lukewarm response to their attempts to engage her, they hid it well. Even when she threw a colossal tantrum when they came to take her out for ice cream, they were understanding and calm. If not that day, then surely the next, Jazzy would feel ready. It was pretty heroic of them to show up day after day when it meant nearly three hours on the road. At last, after five long days of Jazzy's refusing to leave my side when they arrived, I had enough.

"Okay, cookie," I said firmly, "today is the day. Your mom and dad will be here in a few minutes to take you to the store for ice cream. You don't have to like it. You don't have to have fun. You don't have to eat even one lick of an ice-cream cone, but you do have to go. I know you need to scream, so you have about ten minutes, and I want you to start screaming now and get it out of your system. So let's go. Start screaming."

Jazz was caught up short by the demand to holler. The last thing she wanted was to cooperate with me on any of this.

"I don't want to scream," she said in a tone fit for a queen. "I not in the mood."

I had to turn around so she wouldn't catch me smiling.

"I didn't ask about your mood. You like to scream when you don't get your way about things, and you are not getting your way today, so if I were you, I would start throwing a fit. You don't have a lot of time."

"I don't like you anymore," she replied with her little nose pointed straight up in the air.

"You don't have to like me. You have to go out for ice cream."

When the crunch of gravel in the driveway signaled the Hamiltons' arrival, Jazz picked up her coat and stood by the door. With every ounce of dignity a four-year-old could muster, Jazz greeted Al and Barbara.

"Hello, Mommy. Hello, Daddy. I ready to go out today."

And that was that. She didn't always go easily, but she went, first for an afternoon, then for a full day. There was one overnight, then a weekend, and it was over.

There was no funeral, no sympathy cards to acknowledge our grief. It seemed a small thing, I suppose. Natural. Children came. They stayed, and then they left only to be replaced by another child with another sad story. But to us, they were not interchangeable just because there were a lot of them. Jazz was our Jazz. Irritating beyond belief but altogether who she was. For a slice of time, she was ours.

We lost Priscilla the same week. Although her mother was still not well, her father had recovered enough to take her home. It was a very different leave-taking. For one thing, Priscilla was delighted to go home. There was never any doubt that she belonged there or that her parents loved her ferociously. We all missed Priscilla in a general way, but we didn't grieve for her because she never let herself belong to us. She knew who her family was, which is just as it should be.

The beds didn't remain empty for long. We took a sweet little five-year-old with cerebral palsy and learned how to manage full-body braces. Then a hearing-impaired three-year-old taught us the fundamentals of sign language. Both of these were short-term kids, who demand lots of time but no emotional commitment, which was perfect for us.

In between wrestling with braces and figuring out how to insert very tiny batteries into a set of minuscule hearing-aids, I took Karen for her five-year-old checkup. After the usual height, weight, and blood pressure check, I mentioned the tics and the anxiety we were seeing. Dr. Shubach made a note of it but certainly didn't seem concerned.

"Just to ease your mind, I'll give you an appointment with a neurologist, but I suspect this is just a transient tic disorder. They're pretty common in this age group. I'm sure it's nothing to worry about."

I was standing at the receptionist's desk, waiting to pay my bill, when Dr. Shubach came out with a small stack of papers in her hand.

"I ran some information off for you. You might want to read it when you have a minute."

I remember stuffing the papers into my bag in an untidy bundle. I found them later in the day and left them on the counter in the kitchen. I think I glanced at them, but since they looked like nothing more than some Internet articles, I dismissed them as something to make the doctor feel as though she had done something for us.

Bruce came home from work late that night. With Jazz and Priscilla gone, the house was eerily quiet. We chatted for several minutes about his work and my day.

"Hey! How did Karen make out at the doctor's today? Did Dr. Shubach have anything to say about the tics? I was tied up with that roof project and forgot to call."

"It's nothing to worry about. We have to take her to a neurologist, but it looks like a transient tic disorder. It should clear up on its own in a month or two. Dr. Shubach gave me some handouts, if you want to read them. I think I left them in the kitchen."

Bruce must have begun reading them while I called the kids for dinner. He was engrossed enough not to hear me tell him that dinner was on the table. He tucked the papers under his seat. It was a noisy dinner, even though we had only six kids at the table. Angie, Neddy, and Ben were talking about the schedule for spring soccer tryouts. Crystal was full of questions about an overnight campout with her Girl Scout troop. Karen was being silly about her silverware, refusing to eat until she had lined it up perfectly. Daisy was mostly rocking in her seat, trying not to notice the food on her plate. I was talking to everybody at once, rubbing Daisy's back, enjoying the easy camaraderie of Ben and the girls and idly wondering why Bruce was so quiet.

After dinner everyone disappeared to finish up homework or phone calls or showers. That left me alone with the dishes. I made a feeble attempt at a protest, but the kids were aware I was bluffing. I didn't really mind doing the dishes alone. It gave me quiet time to think, something that was at a premium in our house. After the dishes I made a pot of coffee and joined Bruce in the living room. I was surprised to find him still reading the handouts. I had forgotten all about them.

"Those must be a lot more interesting than they look," I said with a smile. "You gave up helping me with the dishes to read them."

"You didn't read them, did you?" He asked with a serious expression that I rarely saw on his face.

"No. Why? Are they interesting?"

He didn't answer right away. He finished the final page and looked up at me with moist eyes. "Hmm," he said finally. "I'll be a son of a gun."

"What is it, Bruce? You look upset."

"Well, I guess I am rather."

"You're scaring me. What the heck is wrong?"

"Lots, apparently. According to this, Karen has Tourette's syndrome."

Six

W hy you look like you gonna cry, Kathy?"
I did feel like crying ever since I had read the information the doctor had given me about Tourette's syndrome. TS
is a chronic neurobiological disorder that causes involuntary
movements and sounds. These tics usually appear between the
ages of five and eight. They often begin with eye blinks and nose
twitches, and the sniffs and hums we were now hearing nearly
constantly from Karen. The tics generally worsen, becoming
the most troubling during the middle school and high school
years, when children are most vulnerable. Tics can be little
more than bothersome, or they can be disabling. Tourette's
rarely appears as a solo act. Obsessive-compulsive disorder is

often present, as are learning disabilities and behavioral problems. There is little in the way of treatment, and no cure. There was a lot more information, but I could absorb only so much before I became overwhelmed and so distraught I could barely breathe.

I managed a small smile for Daisy. She and Crystal had been sadly neglected in the weeks since Karen had seen her doctor. Not in a physical sense, for they were clean and there was always a meal on the table. But I just couldn't muster the energy for the kind of emotional involvement they were used to from me. Bruce did his best to pick up the slack, but he was preoccupied as well. Crystal fared better than Daisy. She was old enough to have other resources. Friends called her for play dates, and Patty took her for at least part of every weekend. But Daisy needed more from me than she was getting.

"I'm not going to cry, Daisy. I just have a lot on my mind."

"Me, too," she said with a small sigh.

That comment jolted me out of my self-absorption.

"What's up, sweetie? Are you okay?"

"I okay. I just wondering about my mom. Is I going home soon?"

"I don't know, Daisy, do you want to go home? You don't talk about it much."

"I miss my mom sometimes, but I be a bad girl at her house. That's why her don't like me. She thinks I weird."

It would have been easy to lie to Daisy just then. Maybe I should have. Some truths are just too hard for a child who was not quite seven. But when I looked at Daisy, I couldn't bring myself to rattle off some hollow words. She had changed in the few months she had spent with us. Her body was still lean, although she was no longer emaciated. She had some color in her cheeks and her hair was filling in. But those were not the biggest changes. It was her eyes that were different. The frantic look that haunted them had been replaced by something else. It wasn't altogether a good change. I thought she looked weary, as though she had seen too much to really be a little girl anymore. But there was acceptance there, too. Daisy was a sprite, a fairy child with one foot in another world, but she was tough, too. She had walked through fire in a few short years, and she was still standing. She needed the truth from me.

"I'm not sure about that, Daisy. Sometimes grown-ups have so many of their own worries to think about that they don't have a lot left over to give to other people, even their own kids. I know your mom cares about you. That's why she's happy to have you here. She knows we love you a lot. I think she wants you to be happy, but she doesn't know how to help you. I wish it was different, but wishing doesn't make it so."

"Is that why you not talking to us anymore? You got too many worries?"

"I guess. But it's not your fault. It's been a long winter, hasn't it? I think we all need spring."

Daisy looked up at me with a smile that didn't quite reach her eyes.

"Will you smile again in the spring?"

"That's a promise, Daisy. I will definitely smile again in the spring."

In spite of my promise, smiles were hard for me to come by, at least in my private moments. But I tried to put on a happy face for Bruce and the kids. Time cast a merciful shadow over the next few weeks. I remember it but not clearly, perhaps because I don't have the strength to live it again. I know I read the hand-outs quickly the first time. Then, after the children were in bed, I read them again, the way one reads a love letter, extracting subtle meaning from every syllable, every mark of punctuation. Denial is, I think, highly underrated as a coping mechanism, although all the literature about grief points to it as a necessary first step with any loss. For the next several weeks Bruce would see Karen wiggle her nose or roll her eyes and, out of her hearing, say in an annoying singsong voice, "Karen has Tourette's syndrome." I would give him a poke in the ribs. "You are such a crepe hanger. She has a transient tic disorder." I always said this with a laugh, as though Bruce was too silly for words.

"Can you stop that?" I asked Karen once when no one else was around.

"I can't, Mommy. I wish I could. It makes it hard for me to look at books. I feel like I got an inside itch."

I called the neurologist suggested by Karen's doctor. I didn't realize how anxious I was to make an appointment and put this talk of tics and syndromes behind me until I was given a time for late November.

"November!" I said, panic too clear in my voice. "My daughter may have Tourette's syndrome! She can't wait that long for an appointment. Don't you have times for emergencies?"

The receptionist was very kind. "Seizures are an emergency. Tics are worrisome, but they aren't dangerous. I'm afraid she'll have to wait."

"Can you recommend another doctor? We'll go anywhere. Boston, even New York if we have to."

"There aren't a lot of pediatric neurologists, ma'am. I can give you some other names, but they all have waiting lists." There was a moment of silence. "I can put you on our cancellation list. If something opens up, we can give you a call."

I took the spot on the waiting list, but I didn't expect much.

Karen knew that her body was behaving in odd ways, but she didn't seem overly concerned. Puzzled, maybe, but unaware of the turmoil her humming, sniffing, and eye rolling was causing the rest of us. Bruce and I had talked to the older kids about Karen's tics and made it clear that they were not to mention them to their sister unless she brought the subject up. She was not to be teased or questioned or made to feel embarrassed. I wasn't worried about the younger bunch. Crystal would follow Angie and Neddy's lead, and Daisy had enough to worry about, just keeping her own fragile self together, to pay much attention to Karen's tics. I certainly worried about September. Kids are notoriously unkind to anyone who steps outside the boundaries of the normal, as evidenced by the treatment of some of my more unusual foster children, and Karen was looking more unusual every day. She added a shoulder shrug to her repertoire of unintentional movements, and a throat clearing as well.

The worry was beginning to consume me. It left little space for much else. When my son Nathan told me that he was considering spending the summer working on a banana boat in South America, I greeted the news with little more than a faint smile and a shrug. Early in April, I decided I had to do something, anything I would find productive and engaging enough to get my mind off Karen and planted somewhere else, even if only for an afternoon.

Painting the ceiling in the room Angie and Neddy shared was perfect. I hate to paint and the ceiling was a disgrace. Since we had all the supplies on hand, I was able to get right into the project without a trip to town. Everyone but Karen was in school. I set her up with crayons and paper in the playroom and got busy.

I was up on a step stool when the phone rang. I let it ring, thinking I would check the machine when I had a minute, forgetting that Karen had just started answering the phone on her own. I could hear her end of the conversation.

"Yes. This is the Harrison residence," she said, sounding as if she had had this receptionist job for years. "She can't come to the phone right now. Who should I say is calling? Just a moment. I'll tell her. Hey, Mom," she yelled, "it's Dr. Gilmore's office. Can you call them back?"

"Jeez! Don't hang up. I'm coming!" I nearly fell off the step stool, wiping paint on my jeans and tripping over the sheet that was doubling as a drop cloth.

"Yes, this is Mrs. Harrison. Yes, Karen's mother. Can we be there in two hours? We can be there in one if we have to. Yes. We have the referral. Thank you! Yes. Of course. Thank you."

I was exaggerating, actually. Two hours was going to be a

stretch. The office was an hour away in light traffic, and I had to scrounge up after-school child care and get Karen and myself presentable. I called Bruce at work before I did anything else, to arrange to meet him halfway so that we could do this together.

Karen was, of course, full of questions. "Why do I have to go to the doctor's if I'm not sick? Why can't I see Dr. Shubach? How come you have white speckles in your hair?"

We had already told Karen as much as we thought she should hear, but I went over it all again. "This is a special kind of doctor, who can help us find out why it is so hard for you to keep your body still and why you make noises that you don't want to make. He won't do anything that hurts. My hair is speckled because I was painting a ceiling."

"Can he make me stop?" Karen looked very serious when she asked this. The worry in her voice brought me up short. I had been so caught up in my own distress that I hadn't focused on how Karen might be feeling about all of this.

"I don't know, baby. I hope so."

A friend agreed to meet the girls' school bus. Bruce and I made plans to meet at the mall, then drive to the doctor's office together. We greeted each other with a hug that lasted a long time. Neither one of us spoke.

We sat in silence for a few minutes until Bruce fiddled with the radio and found a country station with some rockabilly music we all knew and could sing along with. Singing helped pass the time, as we drove through the town and onto the highway and began counting down the exits.

Many cities have a section like the one we entered, with the hospitals forming a small city of their own. There are hospitals for orthopedic problems, others for high-risk pregnancies, and several with units devoted to the ailments of modern living—cancer, diabetes, and trauma. The largest of the hospitals has a fine children's department and is surrounded by offices for the pediatric specialists who have privileges at all the hospitals.

It was strange to be walking through these halls with Karen, Bruce holding her hand on one side and me on the other. We passed children in wheelchairs, eyes glazed and drool staining the front of their shirts. There were children with the obvious stigmata of congenital syndromes, and several with the bald heads and weary eyes of cancer victims. I was unwilling to meet the eyes of their mothers with my lovely, healthy daughter at my side. "I'm so sorry," I wanted to say to these families. "We don't actually belong here. We have a real life at home. I will be happy to make a generous contribution to research, but please don't ask me to become a member of the club."

It was, if anything, worse once we located the office. Clearly, no one came here with one of your basic kid ailments. There were no runny noses or fevers. In fact, ill children were barred form the waiting room. This was a place not for illness but for heartbreak.

In spite of the admonition to be on time, we still waited for nearly a half hour before being called into the examination room. A nurse did the measurements—height, weight, and head circumference—before leading us to a small examination room.

Once again we waited, with Karen getting more anxious by the minute.

We had waited long enough to be startled by the knock on the door. Dr. Gilmore introduced himself and didn't waste any time on small talk. He just asked why we were there. I am sure I am not the only mother to have talked to him in couched terms, hoping to protect her child from the reality of her concerns. Bruce broke in from time to time to clarify a point but remained mostly focused on Karen, trying to distract her so that I would be free to talk to the doctor.

The exam was brief. He spent some time testing Karen's reflexes and looking in her eyes, but mostly he just talked to her. Not about her family history—we already mentioned that she was adopted and we didn't know a lot about her family of origin—but about movies and preschool and her brothers and sisters. I knew why. He wasn't interested in her life. He wanted to watch her tic. And she did. Watching her like this, I was taken aback by how much. At last, he asked Bruce to take Karen to the waiting room. When the office door was shut, Dr. Gilmore took a seat across from me. He folded his hands under his chin and took a breath before he started.

"Karen is a lovely child. I'm impressed with how bright and friendly she is. So, tell me. What do you think is wrong with her?"

"Oh, I know what's wrong with her," I said, as though I had accepted it all along. Maybe I had, because the words came out easily. "Karen has Tourette's syndrome."

Here's the truth of it. You don't get to pick. It isn't a question of if you will cope. You have to cope. What else is there to do?

The initial sadness brought a blackness to my soul that I hope never to experience again. In this blackness I took three showers a day in order to have a place to weep in private. I couldn't eat, couldn't sleep, couldn't read or write. I even avoided church because the music made me cry. It occurred to me at last that my despair was not for Karen. She accepted what we told her about Tourette's and moved on. I knew I had to follow her lead and move on, too. There wasn't space in my life for self-pity. I was able to get mad then, and for a few days I raged against God and the universe and anyone unlucky enough to be in my way. I prayed that if only this thing would go away, I would be a better, kinder person. I would do good works and devote my life to the less fortunate. But it didn't go away. It was here and if I was going to help Karen, I had to let the grief go. I still cried from time to time, but these were cleansing tears and soon over. I bought the books and joined the association and educated myself. I used the lessons I learned from the children, like Daisy, who had come to me over the years with losses and betrayals beyond my comprehension. Children who cried but woke up in the morning and loved again.

Seven

The sounds of shouting and crashing blocks streamed through the front door of the Children's Clinic. Every Monday afternoon I brought Daisy there to meet with her therapist, Toni, for an hour. That's not a lot of time to devote to the rather daunting task of helping weave a child's fragile little self back together, but it's all an insurance company will usually pay for. Fortunately, in spite of a head full of auburn curls and deeply dimpled cheeks that made her look more like a college cheerleader than an expert in early childhood trauma, Toni Tonelli was extraordinarily good at what she did. Actually, there was a bit of cheerleading in it. She kept me focused and motivated to do the day-to-day stuff that was the most helpful to a child who still often refused to eat, panicked at the sound of thunder, and continued to draw graphic pictures of her sexual abuse. I was grateful that Daisy was such a poor artist. As it was, her stick figures made it all too clear what Frank had done to her. I didn't know that I could have stood much more detail.

I wasn't sure what Daisy and Toni did together every Monday afternoon. I didn't ask, and Daisy never offered to talk about it, but I know that after most sessions, Daisy returned to me and collapsed in my lap, looking drained and drawn. Our drive home was often quiet.

The Children's Clinic was one of several local agencies that provided therapy to children. Although the choice of therapist was up to me, the clinic, as it was usually referred to, was always the first place I called. The staff had expertise in all the issues my children were likely to be dealing with. I could always find a therapist who specialized in trauma, sexual abuse, learning disabilities, anxiety disorders, and attachment problems, as well as the more serious forms of mental illness. The waiting room saw kids whose parents were college professors and kids from the homeless shelter. It was an interesting if sometimes unsettling place. Luckily, therapy for children in foster care is paid for by the state-provided health insurance given to all children on the day they are taken into state custody.

The waiting room group of parents and kids who shared the Monday afternoon timeslot was becoming a family of sorts. We were all a little distant at first, worried, I guess, that any familiarity would seem intrusive, but that didn't last. First there was some eye contact, then some shared smiles over some funny things one of the kids did, then, finally, conversation. No one ever asked why someone's kid was being seen. Occasionally, a mother might volunteer some general information, but mostly there was real respect for our kids' privacy.

One afternoon I found myself sitting alone in the waiting room. It was a school vacation day, and apparently the other parents had opted to keep their kids home. Time alone was a luxury for me. I saw Daisy off with Toni and was just settling down with a good book when one of the missing moms, a harried-looking redhead named Valerie, rushed in the door with her little boy in tow. He was a bumper car of a kid, knocking into every wall, toy, and piece of furniture he passed. He was such a little wild man. I'm not sure how much good the therapy was doing him, but I could guess that Mom was glad for the hour-long break from his nonstop action, if nothing else.

"Whew," Valerie said, with a hearty sigh of relief when he was finally escorted upstairs. "He's a good kid, but he sure can take it out of me. I don't ever look forward to no-school days."

I gave a noncommittal smile and buried my head in my book, hoping to break off our conversation.

It was quiet for a moment, then the woman spoke again. "I hope you don't mind me asking, but are you a foster parent?"

That got my attention. I was an inveterate recruiter of new families, and the best advertising was always having people ask about my experiences. I'm afraid that I usually talked about the wonderful parts of fostering and left the horror stories to another day.

"I am," I answered. "How did you know?"

"Well, actually, I know Daisy. At least, I know her family. We lived on the same street when I was growing up, and my mom goes to church with Mrs. Hodges. I heard that Glenna's kid was in foster care, but I didn't believe it. I mean, they aren't the sort of family who has their kids taken, are they?"

I was in a pickle now. It was one thing to talk about foster care in a general way, but because of my confidentiality agreement, I couldn't talk about my kids.

"Not every kid who lands in foster care is taken, and it's not just poor people who have problems. I can't discuss Daisy, but I can say that probably there are people in your own neighborhood, maybe in your own family, who are struggling with their kids. They just don't talk about it."

I may have been unwilling to talk about Daisy, but Valerie clearly had no such problem talking about Daisy's family. I should have stopped her. It would have been easy enough to say that I really couldn't have any conversation about my kids' families and change the subject, but my curiosity got the better of me. In spite of what I had just said, Daisy's family was unique. Kids with families like hers don't usually end up in care. When you have money, education, and connections, there are other resources, other options besides the care of strangers. Foster care has a bad reputation. Often it's well deserved. It is the last resort for most kids.

When Valerie began to tell me about Daisy's family, I put down my book and leaned forward. It didn't take much more than the occasional "Oh, really!" and "How about that" to keep her talking. By the time the kids came back downstairs, I had a much clearer picture of Daisy's family.

Loretta and Howard Hodges had been the perfect couple. They were both lawyers and worked together in the same small firm. They skied in the winter and had a summer cottage on the Cape. The golden couple should have had the golden child. What they got was Glenna.

Not all children are good fits for the parents they have, and that seemed to be the case with Glenna. She was a late-life baby and not at all what the Hodges had expected. She was, by all accounts, a fussy, high-need baby who never progressed as quickly as her parents wanted her to. Much to their embarrassment, she was held back in kindergarten and struggled all through school. She wasn't an athlete or a musician or an artist. In spite of tutoring and every enrichment program the community had to offer, Glenna barely managed to graduate from high school. Things went from bad to worse when her dad died unexpectedly the same year she flunked out of the only college that had been willing to accept her. Her grieving mother found solace in the church, whereas Glenna drifted from job to job, boyfriend to boyfriend, until she found herself pregnant with no husband and no prospects. If her mother had been embarrassed by Glenna before, she was mortified now. Mrs. Hodges did her duty by Glenna. Her reputation wouldn't have stood for her turning her daughter and infant grandchild out on the street, but she wasn't happy about it.

"Glenna was never anything but a headache to her mother,"

Valerie continued. "I have to admit, though—I'm surprised she let Glenna's kid land in a foster home. No offense, but I wouldn't let any kid I cared about go to one."

I let that remark slide. "What about this last boyfriend? Do you know anything about him?"

"Who? Frank? That guy is a piece of work. He's good-looking but a slime ball, if you ask me."

The sound of thundering sneakers signaled the end of therapy for Valerie's son. I was glad for the few minutes I had to myself to think about all I had just heard. I was a little embarrassed to have been so shameless in my curiosity, but I was glad to have the information. It was another little piece of the puzzle that was my Daisy.

I returned home, pleased to find a message from Susan asking me to call her about a couple of kids she needed to place. The call was a relief. Since Karen's diagnosis, I hadn't heard from Susan except for an occasional call to see how we were holding up. The truth was that I needed to get busy. Otherwise, I thought too much. Within the next two weeks, I took in two children I might have otherwise turned down because of their rather extreme special needs. Kayla was an immature fourteen-year-old with a bad attitude and a baby due in just weeks. We were holding on to her only until a bed opened up in a home that took parenting teens.

"Please tell me she doesn't plan to keep this baby," I begged her worker after I met the mom-to-be for the first time. "She's just a kid herself, and not a very well-put-together one."

"Oh, she plans to keep it," said her worker, Doris, a severe-looking older woman, who seemed like a bad match for street-smart Kayla. "It's the thing to do in high school these days." Her face softened a bit. "I've been Kayla's worker since she was seven. Her case should be moved into the adolescent unit, but I hate to lose her now. I'm the only person who's stuck with her. Her mother doesn't want her. Nobody knows who her father is. She's never maintained well in a foster home, and she's had a couple of failed adoption attempts. Why wouldn't she want a baby? At least she'll have somebody to love her. She has no way of knowing a baby is just a big bucket of need. When she finds out, we'll be calling you to take that little one, too."

"Do you want me to suggest adoption to her?"

"There's no harm in trying, but I don't think you'll have much luck."

Kayla joined us, taking the bedroom vacated by Nathan, who had moved into his own apartment.

Maggie came the following week with quite a story from her social worker. Maggie was three. She didn't speak and ate only with her hands. She was found with her six-year-old sister and two baby brothers, living in little more than a shack in the hills. The house had running water and electricity, but that was about it for amenities. It wasn't poverty that removed the kids from their parents—it was neglect. Rarely were the children let out of the house. In spite of the lack of language, none had received early-intervention services. Neither parent could remember the name of the kids' doctor, although they claimed that the children had been immunized at some point. The family was so socially isolated that there is no telling how long they would have escaped detection had not the mother refused to send her oldest child to school, telling school officials who called that she was planning to homeschool her. When an educator dropped by to evaluate the quality of the homeschooling, she was appalled at the conditions in the house and at the bizarre behavior of both parents. She immediately called social services. Since dirt isn't an emergency and the children didn't seem in immediate danger, it took a day or two for them to pay a call. When the workers finally arrived, they were concerned, not just for the children's safety but for their own. Dad was odd but fairly docile. Mom was another story. After a confrontation that had the potential to become very violent, the social workers left without the kids but returned a few hours later with two burly police officers. Apparently it was quite a scene, with dogs barking and Mom screaming and the bewildered children sobbing. While this was going on, Dad followed the social workers around, trying to engage them in a discussion about the Russian agents he was certain had moved in down the road.

Leon, the social worker who delivered Maggie to us, was a young man I had not met before. He was huge, his head nearly grazing the top of the doorway. It was hard to picture this hulking kid being chased around a kitchen by a tiny woman wielding a skillet, but I heard that was what happened. Since he had already taken quite a ribbing in the office about it, I let the subject alone. He looked so exhausted that I offered him a cup of coffee before he set out again.

"I would love to take you up on it, but I have my partner

waiting in the car with other kids. We have to bring them to their foster homes."

"Were you able to place any of them together?"

"These kids are such little terrors that we're lucky to have found placements at all. Together would have been out of the question. I have to tell you, they couldn't pay me enough to do your job. At five, I get to go home."

It didn't take long for me to see what he was talking about.

While we talked, Leon held tight to the back of Maggie's sweatshirt. The minute he let go, she bolted. My kitchen is large with a lot of open space. There aren't really any good hiding places. Maggie headed for the only place that afforded her any protection from us—underneath the table. There she sat, not so much crying as screeching wildly. We have a big table. It seats ten easily and twelve in a pinch. Crouched as she was, right in the middle and holding on ferociously to the chair in front of her, she wasn't going to be easy to dislodge.

I motioned for Leon to go. Maggie undoubtedly associated him with her abrupt removal from home. I was afraid his presence would just make things more difficult. He left without an argument. I take it the car ride had been none too pleasant, and he had already had as much of Maggie as he could take for one day.

With help from one of the kids, I could have pried her hands free while someone pulled her out from behind. But that was hardly the tone I wanted to set for her life with us, especially since she was already a dangerous combination of terrified and furious. If I didn't manage to calm her down soon, I was in for a very long night.

"Hey, Maggie," I said quietly, "this must be pretty scary, coming to a house and not knowing anybody. You must be wondering where your mom and dad went." There was a slight flicker in her eyes when I asked about her parents. "I'll bet you're wondering about your brothers and sisters, too. I would be wondering about them. Lots of kids come here while their families figure out how to take better care of their children. They all worry about their left-behind families."

I thought the volume of the screeching diminished slightly and I continued. "Maybe you can help me. Maybe we can draw a picture of this house for your sister, and she can draw a picture of the house she's staying at for you. I have some crayons you can use."

By this time, the noise had attracted the attention of the other girls. It was nearly four o'clock, and they were all home from school. I had sent them upstairs when Maggie arrived, hoping to keep her from being overwhelmed, but there was no way they were going to stay there with all this excitement.

Kayla crouched down awkwardly next to me. Any hope I held that she might be helpful was short-lived. Although none of my girls had more experience with being small and frightened and alone than she, empathy, it seemed, was too much to expect of her.

"Damn," she said with disgust, "she ain't very cute, is she? I was hoping for a cute one. What's wrong with her eyes? She got something going on there, don't she?"

Karen was going through a stage of correcting the other girls' behavior every chance she had. "That's not very nice, Kayla. Is it, Mommy? Kayla should talk nicer. She'll hurt the sweet little girl's feelings."

Karen reached tentatively under the table to touch Maggie's hand, and the sweet little girl bit her.

Kayla, of course, found that to be the funniest thing since *Seinfeld*. With a brawl threatening to erupt between Kayla and Karen, it was Daisy who came to the rescue. She disappeared upstairs and returned with a stuffed bunny. It was a decrepit old thing, missing an eye and most of its fur, but it did have an air about it. It reminded me of the Velveteen Rabbit, real from being loved so much. We had a huge collection of stuffed animals, all far grander than this one. But this was the bunny the kids wanted when they were sad or sick or in need of a friend, belonging to nobody and everybody.

"Here, girl," said Daisy in her soft lisp, "you can use our bunny. I remember when I felt like you." Daisy's voice was little more than a whisper, and everyone quieted to hear her. "I cried every night, but now I don't. You will feel better. Your mommy will come back."

Maggie grabbed the bunny, tucked it under her arm, and stuck her thumb in her mouth. It was a relief to have the noise stop.

"I want everyone to find something to do. Let's give Maggie a chance to get used to us without hovering around her as if we're the fruit flies and she's the banana."

I hoped that with no audience, Maggie would soon tire of the underside of the kitchen table and decide to join us. Karen slipped in a movie, Crystal started on a puzzle, and Daisy joined Karen on the sofa, but Kayla hung around the kitchen, unable to stay away from Maggie.

"Hey, kid, why don't you quit screwing around and get out here."

Maggie shot daggers at Kayla and pulled the chair closer to her.

"Kayla. I asked you to leave her alone please. Now go find something to do."

"You can't let kids get away with nothin'. I'm not letting my kid be no brat. She's gonna learn early how to behave. I tell her to get out from under the table and she'll do it." Kayla paused for a minute. "I sure hope my kid is cute. I want to dress her up nice, ya know? I don't know what I'd think about an ugly kid."

In truth, Maggie was remarkably unattractive. Her hair was a mousy shade of brown and none too clean. It looked as though she had worn bangs at one time, but they had grown out to that annoying point of their hanging right in her mouth. She was short for three and squat, with tiny eyes and a thin downturned mouth. Her right eye was straight, but the left rested squarely in the inner corner. She was dressed in faded boys' corduroys that were too big for her short frame and sat low enough on her hips to show the top of a grungy cloth diaper. Her pilled purple sweatshirt was too small, and the Mickey Mouse dancing across the front had seen better days. Most distressing was her smell, a nauseating combination of stale urine and cigarette smoke.

"Not all kids are pretty, Kayla, and they all go through times when they don't behave well. Times when they're sick or tired or hungry. The thing about being a mom is that you have to be able to put your child first. If they're sick and you want to go to the mall, well, the mall has to wait. Sick kids belong at home. If they get cranky and oppositional, you can't just yell at them or hit them and expect them to behave. You have to find out why they're acting up and do something about it. I could yank Maggie out from under the table, but that wouldn't help me figure out what she needs or how I can help her. If you decide to raise this baby yourself, then you have to be the grown-up. You have to think about what he needs, not what you need."

"What do you mean 'if'? I already told Doris I'm keeping her! You can't make me change my mind with all that talk about how hard it is to be a good mother. I already heard all that stuff from her. I want this kid. I never had nobody, and now I will. It's gonna be me and Nautica."

"Is that what you decided to name her?" I asked, hoping to diffuse the tension a bit. "I thought it was Shawna."

"I changed my mind. Besides, it wasn't Shawna. It was Shania, after the singer. I'm hoping she'll want to be a movie star or an American Idol."

In one of Bruce's old shirts and stretch pants, Kayla didn't look pregnant. She looked like any other girl you might see on the street and wonder vaguely about. Hair bleached once too often, a few too many piercings, a provocative tattoo. Her appearance begged, "Look at me, please! Think I'm pretty! Notice me!" Now she thought a baby would give her what she desperately wanted. Something to make her special.

"What if it's a boy?"

"It won't be a boy. I want a girl."

Through all of this conversation, Maggie didn't stir. With her thumb in her mouth, she exchanged the screeching for a low growl when I looked in her direction. Otherwise, she was quiet. Because I wanted her to come out and didn't want to drag her, I figured I had better get creative. She was obviously more patient than I, and it was getting on toward supper.

"Hey, guys! Who wants a cookie?" Cookies. Twenty minutes before supper. Sometimes I'm shameless.

Of course, everybody but Daisy wanted a cookie. I doled them out right there on the table. But if I thought an oatmeal cookie was going to entice Maggie, I thought wrong. She didn't budge. It was Crystal who finally hit on a solution I hadn't thought of.

"You stink, kid. Come on out and I'll help you find something clean to wear. You like pretty dresses? Kathy's got a lot of dresses."

Maggie had been under the table for the better part of thirty minutes by now and might have been ready to come out anyway. The dress was just an excuse. Whatever the reason, she emerged, and I was able to get a better look at her. She was sizing me up, too, peering at me from under her veil of filthy hair with her one good eye.

Crystal, bless her, ran upstairs with Karen to find some suitable clothes while I led Maggie toward the bathroom. I say "led," but I use the term loosely. She wouldn't let me touch her. I put my hand on her back and she slapped it away. I wondered how I was going to do all that needed to be done. How was I going to bathe a kid who wouldn't let me touch her? And a head check for lice? That was a necessity, but I imagined she wasn't going to be any more cooperative about that than she was for anything else. She needed her hair washed and her teeth checked. It was a good thing dinner was an easy Crock-Pot meal, which was already prepared.

In the end, I didn't do anything but let Crystal slip her into a dress while standing in the kitchen. I disposed of Maggie's clothes in the trash. I rarely do that. It seems so disrespectful, but this stuff was beyond saving. The dress Crystal chose was a ridiculous thing someone had given us, fluorescent green with lace and bows. It was far too big for Maggie, but her eyes lit up when she saw it. I didn't have the heart to send the girls back for something a little less flashy. Between the dress and worn-out hiking boots, Maggie was quite a vision. At least I managed to get her into a clean diaper, although she wouldn't let me wash her so she still smelled pretty bad when Bruce got home. He took it fairly well, considering we had not actually agreed to take another kid.

Dinner was a fiasco. Karen ticced. Daisy rocked. Maggie would eat only bread and potatoes, and those she shoveled into her mouth as though she had never seen a fork. Crystal spilled her milk. Kayla spent the meal sulking because the teenagers were all out for the evening and she was stuck at home with the little kids.

Bruce smiled at me across the length of the table. "If you were looking for something to take your mind off your troubles, hon, looks like you found it."

I was sitting at the kitchen table the next morning with a

notebook and a pad of paper in front of me, making out yet another long to-do list. I had so much to accomplish in the few remaining weeks of school that I knew if I didn't get organized, something important would be forgotten. On the top of the list was finding a dentist for Maggie. I managed to sneak a look in her mouth the night before. I had seen some pretty bad teeth since becoming a foster parent, but hers were by far the worst. The molars were completely decayed. In fact, not more than four teeth appeared cavity-free. The smell from her mouth was so bad that I suspected at least one of the molars had an abscess. She needed a physical, a referral to the special education department, and clothes. She had come without a stitch. I have a good supply of clothes that will take me through several days, but when a kid comes with nothing but the clothes on her back, it still calls for a major shopping trip. I wondered whether I should be looking for a therapist as well. It would be a challenge to find one willing to work with a nonverbal three-year-old, but since her behavior the evening before had been really difficult, I knew I would need some help in figuring out how to manage her. She didn't sleep, wouldn't get in the bathtub, and bit anybody who annoyed her. I was mulling over all this when I realized that Kayla was standing by my elbow.

"Can I help you?" I asked, trying not to sound annoyed. Kayla demanded a lot of my time. More, in fact, than the younger kids did. She always had complaints: She didn't feel well, the little kids wouldn't leave her alone, the older kids didn't want her to hang out with them. She missed her friends and was sick of not being able to wear nice clothes. It was wearing, but at least it was for only a few more days.

"I don't feel good," she said. "My stomach hurts."

That got my attention. She was eight months pregnant.

"Hurts how?"

"I don't know. Crampy. I thought I might have to go to the bathroom, but I did and it didn't help."

"Go lie down for a while. Dr. Miller didn't want you on your feet too much."

"I've been lying down. I really don't feel good."

She had just gotten the words out when she clutched her stomach and dropped to her knees.

"Ow, ow, ow! Something's wrong, Kathy! I never hurt like this before."

"Karen," I yelled up the stairs. "Bring me my purse. Bruce, could you come upstairs a minute? We have a little crisis here."

Thank goodness it was Saturday and Bruce was home.

"Kayla may be in labor," I said, while grabbing my things. "I need to get her into the doctor's. You'll have to call ahead and let them know I'm coming. Keep an eye on the girls. The number is on the pad next to the phone."

"Are you sure? She isn't due for another three weeks."

"Of course I'm not sure, but she's only fourteen and she's not my kid. I'm not going to be the one to decide. I'd rather go and be wrong than not go and be wrong."

"I guess you're right. Well, I'll hold down the fort here. Oh, jeez. What about Maggie?"

"What about her? She's sleeping now. With any luck, she'll be asleep for another hour or two. After that, you'll just have to manage."

Our small town is a solid thirty minutes from the nearest medical center, where there would be staff on duty on a Saturday. I didn't speed, but I didn't dally either. I had visions of delivering a baby in the front seat of my van.

I was surprised to hear Kayla crying softly. Loud, anguished sobs were more her style. These were real tears, more poignant because she was trying to hold them back.

"What's wrong, Kay? Are you scared?" She sniffed and nodded her head. Then came real tears. "I don't want to do this," she sobbed.

"What? Have the baby?"

"Any of it. I don't want to have this kid. I don't want to raise her. I just want all of it not to happen. It isn't like I thought it would be. I thought it would be fun. It hurts!"

"It's too late to change this, Kayla. Babies have a way of coming even when we aren't ready."

Kayla let out a yelp as another contraction hit.

"This might not be the best time to decide, Kay. Let's take care of getting her born first. Okay?"

A nurse was waiting for us. She whisked Kayla into an examination room and left me in the waiting room. Since I had forgotten a book, I was left to peruse ancient *People* magazines. An hour crawled by while I paced the room, too distracted and nervous to sit still. Other patients came and went, but there was no word about what was happening with Kayla. I imagined that if she was actually in labor, we would already be on our way to the hospital. Still, it was a shock when Kayla walked into the waiting room under her own steam.

"The midwife wants to see you, Kathy. She's back here."

Back here was a tiny cluttered office. A woman talking on the phone nodded for us to take a seat while she finished speaking and hung up.

"Hi. You must be Kayla's mom."

"No, but I am responsible for her. I'm Mrs. Harrison. What's going on?

"Kayla is having some Braxton Hicks contractions. They're pretty common in the last month. I told her that this was her body's way of getting ready to have a baby. She should be able to manage the pain without taking anything. I know she's been told to stay off her feet, but sometimes light exercise helps. I spoke to her doctor. She has an appointment on Wednesday. I expect she'll be fine until then. I did an exam, and it doesn't look as if anything is imminent. That can change, of course. If she looks a lot more uncomfortable, by all means bring her back. But I really don't think this baby is ready yet."

The ride home was pretty quiet. I think Kayla was a little embarrassed to have made such a fuss. I thought that this might be a good time to talk about her plans. At least we wouldn't be interrupted in the car.

"Now that things are a little calmer, I wondered if you wanted to talk about your plans. Are you having second thoughts about keeping the baby?"

"I don't know. When I talk to my friends, they're so excited and jealous of me. Abby and Talia are my two best friends. We been in and out of foster homes together a bunch of times. They both can't wait to have a kid. They said welfare will help you get an apartment and a refrigerator and everything. But then I think about being at Donna's house and I don't know. She had a foster baby there, and I got stuck taking care of him. He cried all the time. Even at night. And he puked and got shitty pants and it wasn't fun at all."

"A lot of taking care of a baby is work. What about later? Have you ever given any thought to what you might want to do with your life?"

Kayla looked embarrassed. "I really want to be a model. My friends say I'm pretty enough."

I thought it best to leave that statement alone for now.

"What about the baby's father? You never mention him. What does he think about becoming a dad?"

"How would I know?" Kayla answered with a small shrug. "I haven't talked to him in a while. I think he moved to Florida with his brother."

"What do you plan to do about birth control?" I asked this a little nervously. It wasn't really my business, but I could only hope that if Neddy or Angie were in this same position, some other mom would bring up the subject with them. I thought this was one issue where everybody who cared about children had to take some responsibility.

"I talked to my doctor about getting some pills."

"Do you think that's a good idea, Kayla? You have a hard

time remembering your vitamins. Birth control pills work only if you remember to take them every day."

"I asked her about one of them IUD things, but she said I was still too young for one."

"I have a thought." I rushed ahead before I lost my nerve. "Maybe you could not have sex for a while. Maybe you could wait until you find someone who cares about you. Then you could decide when you were ready to have a family together."

Kayla looked at me as if I were speaking a foreign language. In a way, I was.

"Come on, Kathy. You know I'm not gonna do that. I'd never get a guy if I didn't do it with him."

I took a deep breath before I answered. Angie was a year older than Kayla. I guessed it was time for me to talk to her about life in high school.

"Maybe you could talk to your doctor about a patch then. At least you wouldn't have to remember anything. They're good for three months."

I returned home to find that things had not gone well in my absence. Maggie had bitten Bruce. Daisy had thrown up her lunch. Crystal remembered an afternoon Girl Scout party that she was supposed to make cookies for. She was upstairs pouting because Bruce said she couldn't go until I returned home. The toilet was backed up, courtesy of Maggie and a washcloth. Bruce was tight-lipped and still mopping up the bathroom floor.

"Could you take her while I finish up?" he asked tersely. "I'm afraid to let her out of my sight. She did this while I was washing the crayon marks off the bedroom wall, and she did that while I was fishing the baseball out of the fish tank."

I fastened Maggie into the high chair, where she couldn't cause too much trouble. Within a few minutes, Crystal was dressed for her party, and Kayla was making lunch for herself. I settled Daisy on the sofa with a book and a bucket, then found some cookies in the freezer for the party. I thought it best to avoid Bruce for a bit.

The last thing I felt like doing was packing up a bunch of kids and driving Crystal to a party, but I didn't see any way out of it. I couldn't leave Bruce to mind Maggie again. He had precious few hours outside work to take care of the multitude of chores that the renovation and upkeep of a very old house demanded, and Maggie needed constant supervision. Since Daisy wasn't feeling up to going and Kayla needed a nap, I took Karen and Maggie with me. At least Maggie would be relatively immobile in a car seat.

Because our town was too small to support a scout troop, we had banded together with two other small towns to form one large troop. The upside was that it meant Crystal had a chance to be friends with girls from outside of school. Although she never complained, I know Crystal felt her status of foster child rather keenly. Everyone in class knew that she didn't live with her own family. It was often painful for her, especially those times when she had to miss activities because she had a visitation. In her troop, Crystal was a little more anonymous. The subject of being in a foster home just didn't come up. The downside was that I had to drive.

After a few wrong turns, we found the house we were looking for. I had barely stopped the car before Crystal had the door open.

"Thanks for the ride, Kathy. I'll see you at six."

"Not so fast, kiddo. I haven't met Megan's parents. I want to go in and introduce myself."

"That's okay. I'll tell them you said hello."

"Crystal, I promise I'll try not to do anything to embarrass you in front of your friends, if that's what you're afraid of. But I am going in. I'm not about to drop you off at the home of a stranger without stopping in to meet them."

There wasn't much she could do about it. I was already halfway up the walk with her.

A gaggle of girls greeted Crystal at the front door. There was the usual third-grader round of squeals and giggles. I handed Megan's mom the cookies with one hand and held out my other.

"Hi, I'm Kathy Harrison. Thanks for having the girls over. You're braver than I am."

"Braver or dumber." She laughed. "It's a tough call. I'm Judith. My husband, Charley, is in the family room, setting up the Ping-Pong table. Do you have a minute to come back and say hello?"

"I don't really. I've got the kids in the car. Maybe when I pick Crystal up. Six o'clock. Right?"

"That's right. Thanks for the cookies."

Crystal was leaving the room, arm in arm with a couple of girls I didn't know.

"Hey, Crystal. Aren't you going to say good-bye?"

She looked intensely uncomfortable. "Uh, sure. Bye, Mom." She ran back for a quick hug. Never, not once in the year she had been with us, had Crystal ever referred to me as anything but Kathy. Not even by accident. This was no mistake. Her eyes pleaded with me not to give her away.

"Bye, sweetie. I'm not sure if it will be me or Dad who picks you up, but one of us will be here at six. Have fun."

She smiled broadly. "I will."

Names are important things. They give information, not just about who we are but about who we are to each other. The relationship of foster child to foster parent is fuzzy. I do all the things a real mom does for her kid. I wipe dirty bottoms and snotty noses and never remember to wear gloves because moms don't wear gloves when they do those things. I help with homework and punish kids who are acting up. I bake birthday cakes. I remember that Francesca likes raisins in her oatmeal and that Carlos is afraid of spiders. I accept the compliments when one of my kids hits a home run, as though I had something to do with it. But I always know and, more important, the kid always knows that I'm just the understudy. I'll do, but just until the real thing comes along. I have some moments when I feel jealous. It feels terrible when a kid I have agonized over for months gives her mom, her real mom, the one who can't be bothered to show up for a visit, a handmade card for Mother's Day and forgets to make one for me. I understand it, but I don't have to like it. I felt as if Crystal had just given me a gift. She trusted me and that's a very special thing.

Bruce had regained his good mood by the time I got home.

Daisy and Kayla had both slept, and he was able to repair a pesky electrical problem in the cellar. I got supper in the oven, and we took glasses of wine and sat on the deck for the first time since the previous fall.

We talked over the day, rehashing conversations and sharing Maggie stories.

"She's pretty hard, isn't she," I commented.

"She sure is. Are you going to be able to handle her? She won't be in preschool until September, and they won't take her then if she isn't toilet-trained."

"Even if she isn't trained, I think they'll have to take her in a special needs slot. She has no speech at all. Did I tell you I spoke to her worker yesterday? They assigned Cicely Ryan to the case. It looks like they aren't fooling around on this one. It's going to legal on Monday. They're making the goal adoption for all the kids."

"I thought they had to wait six months and give the parents a chance to use some services."

"Usually they do. But it turns out that the parents already lost two kids about eight years ago for all the same stuff. This time they don't have to wait. I can manage until then. In a way, I think she's kind of cute."

Bruce looked at me skeptically. "You're kidding."

"I don't know. You have to give a kid like her credit. Facing all of us big people and not giving an inch. I wouldn't have done it. I would have been so scared at three, I would have been doing handstands to make people like me. It's kind of endearing."

"If you say so. She has to have a bath tonight. She really smells."

"Are you volunteering?"

"Not me," said Bruce. "That's your department. Besides, I've already been bitten once today. It's your turn."

"Have you noticed something?" I asked Bruce a couple of minutes later. "We've been talking for twenty minutes and neither one of us has mentioned Tourette's syndrome. I guess that's a good sign. It isn't all I think about anymore. I have the energy to think about the rest of my life."

Bruce left to pick up Crystal, having been clued in by me not to say anything if she called him Dad. I decided to tackle the bath for Maggie. I have had any number of children who have resisted getting in the tub. Some kids have been abused in tubs, held underwater or made to sit in water far too hot or cold for comfort. It's a commonplace for sexual abuse to happen, too. Some kids just don't have any experience with tubs. When folks talk about poverty in distant lands, I wonder if they know that in their own towns, among the classmates of their own well tended children, are probably a few for whom soap and hot water are a luxury.

I worked on gathering Maggie up. She was both quick and determined. I knew that if I had to stop to fetch pajamas or locate a bottle of shampoo, I would lose her. Chasing after her was a chore I didn't want to face after a long day. I ran the water, only inches deep, and raided my cooking drawer for novel toys. An eggbeater, a funnel, and all of my measuring cups and spoons found their way into the bathtub so often that I really should have broken down and purchased a set just for the kids.

I would have liked to pop another kid in the tub with Maggie, but I didn't have a kid available. Maggie was beginning to act interested in what the others were doing, and another child might have alleviated her fears somewhat. Crystal was too old. Puberty was approaching at breakneck speed, and she had graduated to the shower. Since Karen had developed a number of the obsessive-compulsive symptoms that usually accompany Tourette's syndrome, she would have found sharing a bath excruciating. Daisy wouldn't have complained because Daisy never complained. With her history of sexual abuse, however, being undressed around any of the others was out of the question. I made a big deal out of her right to keep her body private. That left only me to help Maggie in the tub. Nothing was to be gained from putting it off any longer.

Luring Maggie into the bathroom was a challenge. She wouldn't come when I called her and wouldn't take my hand so that I could lead her. I wasn't even certain that she understood what I wanted, since she responded to any request with either a blank stare or a screaming fit. This time it was the stare, for which I was grateful. Her screams could shatter glass.

"We're going to the bathroom, Maggie," I said firmly, as though I didn't expect an argument. "Can you walk by yourself, or do you need help?"

Maggie stood still as stone, her pudgy hands balled into tight little fists and her mouth pursed tightly. I bent down and put my face even to hers.

"Maggie. Sometimes when an unpleasant thing has to happen, it's best to get it over with as quickly as possible. We are going to the bathroom. You can walk or I can carry you. What's it going to be?" This was a gamble. I wasn't positive I could carry her down the stairs if she really threw a fit.

Maggie met my eye and didn't flinch. I didn't have a choice now. I set the limit and I had to follow through. I picked her up football style. Maggie tried to squirm and wiggle from under my arm, but I had a good grip.

"Sorry, kiddo," I said through gritted teeth, as I hitched toward the stairs. "You had your chance."

"Walk!"

The word was gravelly but clear and very loud.

"You want to walk?" I asked the question nonchalantly, but inside I was singing. A real word!

"Okay, so walk." I put her down and stood arms akimbo. And she walked. Actually, she flounced, glaring and making sure to stay a full arm's length ahead of me. But she was walking all the same.

When we reached the bathroom, she hesitated. Up until now I had changed her, dressed her, done the very little she would allow in her room. She had never actually been in the bathroom except to wreak havoc with the washcloth.

"Same deal, Maggie. You are getting out of your clothes. You can take them off or I can. Which would you prefer?"

"Me."

"Okay."

She was able to get her things off with a little help. There she stood, naked, with arms folded over her chest and a stare that was glacial.

I took a softer stance with the water, bending over and playing with the eggbeater.

Maggie was such a brave, proud little thing. She hated to act interested, but clearly she was.

"Would you like a turn?" I asked, twirling the eggbeater and churning up a pile of suds.

Her nod was so slight, I would have missed it had I not been looking for it.

"Here. Just turn this. See what the water does. Look! You made a typhoon!"

Maggie's turning was clumsy. I doubted she had much experience with this sort of play, but she managed well enough to whip the water impressively. She spied the funnel and picked it up to examine the small hole, not realizing it was full of water.

"Oops. You got a face full, didn't you? Here. Why don't you climb in? Then it won't matter if you get wet."

She didn't jump in with any enthusiasm, but she did lift one foot over the edge, testing the water. Then, very gingerly, she put her other foot in. She stood there shivering for a few seconds and finally sat with a plop in the shallow water.

"That's not so bad, is it? I like baths. I like to play in the water and become clean and good-smelling." I said all of this softly, while ever so gently soaping her back. When she didn't protest, I lathered her arms and then her legs.

The water was gray in minutes. I moved my hand to let out

the dirty water and replace it with clean. She stopped dead at this unexpected movement. I had never seen a child so vigilant. I went back to my monologue about the water and the soap and how well she was doing. Her hair was next. It was as dirty a head as I had ever run across, and I had seen some filthy ones. It wasn't just her hair that was foul. Her scalp was encrusted with grime, and there was a nasty-looking crust behind each ear. I ran my hands through her hair, wetting it without actually pouring water over her. I lathered her head with baby shampoo, letting it sit to dissolve the caked-on dirt. She hadn't spoken while in the tub. I wondered if she might, now that the ice was broken.

"Have you ever had your hair washed, Maggie?"

She nodded, but I made sure I was looking elsewhere.

"I'm sorry, Maggie. I didn't hear you. What did you say?"

I waited for an answer. Sometimes parenting is all about timing.

"It washed."

I hadn't been expecting this. A full sentence, soft but clear. I sat with an idiot grin on my face, delighting in this not-so-small victory.

It took three washes before Maggie's scalp looked clean. The time in the tub was long enough to soak the accumulated sludge from under her nails and off her feet, too. When I finally lifted her out, she was waterlogged but squeaky clean. The other children were putting together a block castle. Even Kayla was engaged, so I took advantage of the time. Fifteen minutes later Maggie boasted a new haircut and even a halfhearted job of brushed teeth. She looked so sweet. Not pretty, exactly—it was going to take more than a bath to accomplish that—but like a typical kid, which was even better. The change wasn't just the bath or the haircut, although both certainly helped. The real change was in her expression. For the first time since her arrival, Maggie was smiling.

Eight

"Presenting the beautiful princesses!"

Karen, Daisy, and Maggie pirouetted into the living room, visions in thrift-store finery and aluminum-foil crowns. They were an unusual trio for royalty. Maggie, short and boxy, was wearing what I think was at one point a slip. It was held up with a leopard-print belt and topped with a shiny purple square-dance blouse and no fewer than a half-dozen sets of Mardi Gras beads. Karen had scrounged up her costume from one of the older girls' ballet recitals. It was the usual concoction of tulle and sequins and was embellished with a feather boa. As charming as the other two looked, it was Daisy who stole the show. She had managed, with the help of a large safety pin, to hold up the skirt of what must have been the world's ugliest pink bridesmaid's dress. Her top was from a negligee, black and quite chic. She was the only one not wearing a crown, opting for the more fetching look of a velvet hat, complete with some large, hideous fake flowers. All three girls had on so much costume jewelry, it was a wonder they could walk. The folks from the Salvation Army store were probably delighted to get rid of the stuff, but I'm sure they questioned, if not my sanity, then at least my taste.

Bruce and I were enjoying a rare midweek show. He was on vacation, and the girls were just out of school for the summer.

A lot had changed in just a few short months. Crystal was no longer with us. This was one of those cases in which nothing had improved with her mom since Crystal had come into care, but nothing was worse either. Her worker couldn't justify keeping her with us any longer. On the last day of school, Crystal packed her things for the return home. I think it was bittersweet for her. She loved her mother and a part of her loved the life there, too. It was less rigid than life at my house, more spontaneous, probably a lot more fun in an exciting if occasionally dangerous way. But it was less predictable, too. Meals and bedtime would happen when they happened. No one was going to make sure her home-work was done. There would be no more scouts or Sunday school. Ice-skating and sledding would be replaced by hanging out at the mall. Patty made a fun older sister, but that wasn't what Crystal needed. I feared this would not be the last time Crystal would land on the doorstep of a stranger.

Kayla was gone, too. She had been accepted into a program

for parenting teens and had given birth to a son a week later. I visited her in the hospital just after delivery. She was still groggy from the pain medication but elated at the prospect of being a mom. Elation lasted only until reality stepped in. By the time her little one was a month old, Kayla was finished playing house and ready to sign a surrender. I was delighted for the baby; he deserved a grown-up for a parent. But I worried about Kayla. I thought possibly her own troubled history had given her an easy-come, easy-go attitude about having children.

Maggie, the kid we were not at all sure we were up to caring for, had become a family favorite. She was a challenge—obstinate, grumpy, and particular about everything from how her socks felt to the temperature of her food. I have no idea how she managed in a family that barely functioned above the subsistence level. I suspect she shut down when things became too chaotic, but in a rich environment that was used to making accommodations for the quirkiness of its varied members, she thrived, learning at a pace that was exciting for a teacher who sometimes missed the thrill of teaching. By her second week, when she discovered that eating with her hands meant losing her dinner, Maggie had struggled to learn the finer points of using a fork and spoon. The biggest change was her eyes. A patch and glasses had pulled her wandering eye back into alignment. The difference was dramatic. Not only could she see, but the glasses gave her an adorable, bookish look. Homely Maggie was downright cute.

Daisy continued to soar. She had an unexpected flair for the dramatic. These impromptu skits were her doing. She had done remarkably well in school, was able to keep up with first-grade work, and used outside help only for the trouble she had processing language. Although eating was still an issue, she managed most things and had put on six pounds of much-needed weight. She talked only occasionally about living with Frank. My gut told me there was a lot I didn't know, maybe a lot even Daisy wasn't sure about. If I had learned anything about sexual abuse, however, it was that kids deal with what they are ready to deal with when they have the resources to cope and not before. Visits with Glenna were going better. There had been a few overnights and even one long weekend. I wonder now, although I didn't allow myself to wonder then, if there might have been more visits, more overnights, if I had encouraged them.

Foster parents often have more control over these things than one might think. A social worker may supervise twenty-five families. Not all of the children in every family are in foster care, but a lot of them are. Between supervising and transporting to visitations, attending court and clinical conferences, attempting to access services such as housing and mental health, along with the endless paperwork, there is precious little time for simple case management. Sometimes a vigilant foster parent can be instrumental in making sure things get done.

This was one time I was not vigilant. I never called to suggest a visit or to attempt to involve Glenna in Daisy's life any more than I had to. I hated to have Daisy away, especially overnight. I felt as if I were missing an arm when she was gone.

It happens and I don't know anyone who can explain it. A child walks in the door and that child belongs to you. The odd thing is that it is seldom the kid you would expect it to be. It's not the prettiest or the brightest or the best behaved. Sometimes it's the kid who is the neediest, the one you have to spend the most time with. And sometimes it's like falling in love. Inexplicable chemistry.

And finally, Karen. In spite of her tics, obsessions, and compulsions, she was a happy kid. The three little girls were a great match. They were all odd, but that was their magic together. Many times school was a challenge, socially if not academically, but home was always a haven. Here, no one was teased about behavior they couldn't control.

We had been joined by two new children, two beautiful African-American children who were brother and sister. The oldest, Jamal, was just two, and the little girl, Lorrell, a newborn. It made for a full house, especially since Jamal had the energy level of a power plant, and the baby was born cocaine-addicted and cried pretty much all the time. I hoped for short-term for these kids. They were expensive in terms of time, and the other kids were still pretty needy. Their mother was an addict and had not been seen since the kids were taken into care. I knew the search was on for an adoptive family that wanted both kids and was up for a low legal risk.

Bruce and I had settled in to watch the girls' performance, when we were interrupted by the phone. I was feeding Lorrell; Bruce was holding a wiggly Jamal in his lap.

"It's four o'clock, Kathy. Are you sure you want to answer that?"

"I think it's okay," I said. "I've already got a waiver for these two. Home-finding is never going to give me another one."

"Hey, Kathy, it's Evelyn. Are you sitting down?" Those were not words I liked hearing from Daisy's worker.

"I'm sitting. What's up?"

"Glenna just called. She is rescinding the voluntary. She would like to have Daisy packed and ready to leave on Friday."

My stomach did a nasty rumble. "Can she do that? Just call and say she wants her back?" I was trying to remain calm, but my voice betrayed me. The girls stopped their dance routine. They were all too hypervigilant for me to get away with much.

"It's been voluntary all along, Kathy. She can do anything she wants."

"Something must have happened. She hasn't said a word about this to me. I see her every week." It occurred to me that Daisy was going to figure out what I was talking about if I didn't distract her. "Hey, girls, it's too nice to be inside. I want you to go get dressed. It's cool, so put on your sweaters. We'll take the baby for a walk." I heard the chorus of complaints. "The first one down gets the first turn at pushing the carriage." That got them moving, and I returned to the phone.

"Did I do something? Isn't she happy with Daisy's care?"

"Actually, I think she may be too happy with Daisy's care."

"Meaning?"

"Meaning I think she would be happier if Daisy seemed a little more homesick. You're a tough act to follow for a mother who isn't exactly June Cleaver."

"Give me a break, Evelyn. So this is it. She's done being overwhelmed and wants to be a mommy again, and we say good-bye and you bring me another kid."

"That's kind of the way it works, Kathy. This is foster care. It isn't supposed to last forever because you fall in love with a kid. I hate to break it to you, but this isn't about you. It's supposed to be about Daisy." I felt my face flush. I knew the reason the words stung was because they were true. I had let my feelings for Daisy cloud my judgment about what was in her best interest. Of course she needed to go home. It really should have happened a long time ago. I found myself counting on my fingers. Daisy had been with us for seven months! Where the heck had seven months gone?

"What's the plan?"

"Toni Tonelli will keep seeing Daisy. She doesn't think Daisy is at all ready to testify about the sexual abuse. She's such a little space shot, she may never be able to do it. Glenna is in a group for mothers whose children have been molested. Life goes on. There will be another kid, Kathy."

I know she meant to be kind, but I was too upset to hear it just then. "There won't be another Daisy."

Bruce didn't ask about the conversation. He didn't have to. He just moved to the couch and pulled me close, Lorrell nestled between us. After a few moments I began to ease Lorrell into a bunting for her walk, trying very hard not to wake her. Maggie was the first one down, followed closely by Karen. Both girls were wearing overalls and T-shirts and carrying their sweaters.

"What's keeping Daisy?" I asked when she hadn't appeared a few minutes later. "I don't want the baby to get overheated."

"I am here," she answered, coming into the room at just that moment. I stopped short when I saw her. "Daisy, honey. What are you wearing?"

"My sweaters."

"All of them?"

"You said to. You said, 'Girls. Put on your sweaters,' so I did. But I am very hot, and Karen and Maggie don't got their sweaters." Daisy stuck out her lip in a pout. She looked so funny. She was wearing four sweaters, which made it impossible for her to lower her arms. The top one was a bright orange castoff I was keeping for its Halloween-costume potential. I handed Lorrell to Bruce and wrapped Daisy up in a giant hug. "I absolutely said that, Daisy. Sometimes I just don't think. What I meant was, 'Would each of you girls wear a sweater.' I just got confused. Let's pick one of these to wear and we'll go for that walk."

I write a lot about children leaving. I write about the grief mostly because that piece is always there. What I write less about is the second-guessing I indulge in. I think back to all of the mistakes I made. I remember the times I was short-tempered or impatient or dismissive of a child's feelings. In the midst of a busy day, it is very easy to justify those moments, but unfolded laundry is no excuse for not listening when a child needs to talk. Seven months with a family is a long time to sit on something as significant as being sexually abused. Other than the time I found the pictures, Daisy had never volunteered any information about her experience. She never brought it up, never acted it out with her dolls, never drew another picture that I was aware of. As I packed Daisy's things, I wondered if I had missed something important because I had so many other things to think about. Had there been times when she wanted to talk? Had I missed the moment because I wasn't listening? Not knowing gnawed at me with each sock I matched and every book I rescued from under her bed. This could have been, I realize, all a giant self-indulgent excuse. If I spent my time in a futile search for lost opportunities, then maybe I wouldn't have the time to think about life without Daisy.

Bruce and I told her together that night. We tried to make it seem a joyful thing and cause for celebration, but we weren't fooling anyone, certainly not Daisy.

"We'll miss you, Daisy. I hope your mom will let you call us and come to visit sometimes." The words were hard for me to choke out.

"Jazzy don't come. You said she would, but her don't."

Daisy was right. We did think that Jazzy would visit, but that had not happened in a long time. The few times she had come after moving in with her new family had been awful. She had screamed when it was time to leave and refused to get in the car to go back home. Her parents had decided that it was just too hard for her, that there could be no more contact until she was comfortable and happy with them. Unfortunately, she was still having a hard time. She was not sleeping well and having tantrums for hours every day. I talked to the Hamiltons often. They were certainly committed to Jazzy, but their voices sounded tense. I knew that after six months they were beginning to wonder if she would ever settle in.

I pulled Daisy close to me. Her body still felt so fragile in my arms, as if it would break if I held on too tightly.

"I won't forget you, Daisy. Even if I don't see you, I will always think about you."

I spent the next few days preparing for Daisy to go home. I packed her clothes and books and toys. I had her school records transferred and scheduled her for her monthly weight check. Part of the getting ready was also teaching her how to make a long-distance collect call. I had to send her home, but I didn't have to send her without doing what I could to give her a safety net.

The final good-byes were hard. Karen and Daisy clung to each other until I had to pry them apart. Bruce tried to be stoic; he knew that if he cried, that would be it for me, but still he choked up when he scooped Daisy up for one last hug. Even the teenagers, used to the coming and going of so many children, found it impossible to take this one lightly.

I brought Daisy home to Glenna. Evelyn would have done it, but I declined her offer. Since Bruce was home to see to the other children, I was able to go without an entourage. It was a quiet trip. Daisy rode with her head against the side window, tracing the paths of raindrops chasing each other down windowpane hills. She seemed disinclined to talk. I was grateful for the silence. Some kinds of sad are too big for words. I had been able to do so little for Daisy. She could swallow apple juice now. She managed to get her teeth cleaned. She had tubes in her ears. Her education plan was working. She used a tissue. But these were the mechanics of parenting. About the bigger things in her life—things like extracting justice—I was able to do nothing.

Evelyn was right, of course. Life did go on but the grief didn't go away. If anything, it got worse, intensified because we had no way to check on Daisy. Bruce was distraught. Until she was gone, I'm not sure he realized just how important Daisy had become to us. Not a day went by that he didn't call to ask if I had heard from her. In church, when we had an opportunity to ask for special prayers for loved ones, it was Bruce who always asked for a prayer for Daisy.

A rather obnoxious young couple was chosen to adopt Jamal and Lorrell and began daily visitations with us. Tim and Janet Washington had no other children, and I think Jamal scared them with his nonstop energy and cocky little attitude. They countered with a rather punitive approach to every small infraction of the rules. Jamal was a big boy for two, but I thought they were expecting too much of him. Both new parents were crazy for Lorrell. I could see the potential for a problem with good-kid, bad-kid syndrome. Mom, in particular, seemed inclined to play favorites; Jamal responded to her less and less as the days went by. When the pattern was too evident to ignore, I called the children's worker. It took four days for Claudia McPherson to return my call.

"I think you're being a little critical, Kathy," was her response to my apprehensions. "This is a young couple. They can't be expected to be perfect parents."

"I'm not criticizing. I'm just concerned. I was hoping you could talk to them about the way they handle Jamal. I don't know him well, but Bruce and I have found that he responds better to positive consequences for good behavior than he does to punishment. A lot of what they get angry with him for is just kid stuff anyway. Two-year-olds are messy, noisy, busy little things on a good day. And Jamal has had a difficult time. Some of his business is anxiety. Making him sit in a chair for five minutes every time he runs in the house isn't going to help."

"Look. I really want these kids to have an African-American family. This is the only black couple we have on the waiting list who will take two kids. I'm not about to sabotage a perfectly good placement by second-guessing their parenting style."

Claudia was one of the few social workers I worked with whom I just didn't like. I'm sure the feeling was mutual. She thought I was a busybody, who overstepped my boundaries. I thought she was lazy, preferring to call me after visits rather than taking the time to do the supervision herself. On those rare occasions when she actually showed up, she spent most of her time complaining about how her busy schedule kept her from making visits. I didn't have a lot of sympathy. If the people who complained about their lack of time stopped whining and got to work, the time problem would take care of itself. But grousing about Claudia was good for me. It kept me from worrying about Daisy.

Two weeks went by without a word from Glenna. I called a few times, but always got the machine and my messages went unanswered. I stopped calling, although I did check in with

Evelyn. She had not heard from Glenna either. Officially, the case was closed, unless Glenna asked for services. Evelyn had no authority to drop in.

"Let it go," I reminded myself over and over in the weeks after Daisy left. "You gave her what you had to give, and it's time to move on." Some days I even took my own advice.

The past winter had been a hard one. Snow piled up in tall drifts, ice coated the roads, and the temperature hovered around zero. Bruce was concerned about the amount of time I spent on back roads with a pile of kids in the car. There were many times a careless move would have left me stranded several miles from the nearest phone. I kept a well-stocked emergency kit in the back of the car, but I still felt pretty vulnerable. As soon as they came on the market, Bruce purchased a car phone for the van. What we hadn't counted on was that the same isolation that kept us from good television and radio reception also prevented us from being able to use the car phone in all but a few locations. As a result, it remained a silent, useless, black eyesore, good for little beyond being a convenient place to set my gloves. I used it so seldom, in fact, that when it rang for the first time ever in the parking lot of the supermarket, I was so startled, I couldn't remember how to get the receiver out of the cradle. I fumbled around, pushing buttons and swearing under my breath.

"Hello," I finally answered, flustered.

"Hey! It works!"

"I guess. As long as I never have to leave the parking lot, I can talk as much as I like. What's up?"

"Are you coming right home after shopping?"

"I wasn't planning to. I need to pick up some school supplies and a backpack for Maggie. Is something wrong?"

"I guess that depends on your perspective. I got a call from hotline. They just picked Daisy up at the hospital. They want to know if we'll take her."

Nine

⁊

"You didn't get the groceries, did you?" Bruce asked when I pulled in the driveway thirty minutes after his phone call.

"Did you really think I was going to?"

"No. I probably shouldn't even have called you. The social worker is going to take Daisy home to pack her things before they bring her back, so you have plenty of time."

"What happened? Why was she in the hospital?"

"Her mom brought her into the emergency room. She said Daisy was out of control. She wanted a psych intake and some meds. I guess Daisy was hitting Glenna and climbing all over the furniture, like a madwoman. When Glenna told the hospital staff that Daisy spent the last several months in foster care, they called social services to find out what the scoop was. Evelyn is out until Monday, but they sent over another worker who remembered Daisy and knew she'd been with us. She called me. I told her we'd take Daisy until Evelyn got in on Monday and we would figure out what to do next."

"How did Glenna get her to the hospital?"

"In an ambulance, if you can believe it."

My poor Daisy, afraid of both hospitals and sirens. Fear alone would have made her look crazy by the time she got to the emergency room. If a fast-thinking nurse hadn't called social services, no doubt Daisy would be on a locked unit right now.

"Let's not ask her anything," I suggested. "Let's just welcome her back and let her talk when she's ready. She must have an appointment with Toni on Monday. That's soon enough. For now, I think she just needs to feel safe."

What was I expecting when I heard the car pull into the driveway? A kid who had just been through the psychological mill, complete with sirens, a hospital, and men in white coats, aside from whatever had gone on before—all enough to send even a perfectly normal kid over the mental edge. I expected to see what I was feeling—disorganized, confused, fearful.

The car had barely stopped before Daisy was out. She didn't just run up the driveway. She flew, straight into my arms. She was so light, I was able to lift her right up, spin her in a great circle, and pull her close for a hug.

"Hey, kiddo! Welcome home! I have been missing you!"

"Why didn't you never call me? You said you would."
Daisy's voice held no accusation.

"We called. We called lots of times, but I guess you were out.
Didn't you get my messages?"

"My mom said you were too busy with new kids to call me.
She said you probably didn't have time to talk."

"Was I ever too busy for you, Daisy?"

Daisy smiled up at me and shook her head. She looked terrible. Her eyes were surrounded by deep, dark circles, as though
she hadn't been sleeping well, and there was an unhealthy pallor
to her skin. Her hair was thin and wispy. I wondered if she was
pulling it out again. She looked nearly as bad as she had when
she arrived the previous winter.

"Bruce and I need to talk to the social worker, sweetie.
Would you go up and see Karen? I just told her you were coming back, and she's getting your room ready for you. She has
missed you so much."

Daisy ran into the house as though the last month had never
happened. I didn't see any of the emotions I expected. Daisy
didn't look particularly upset or sad or angry. She might have
just returned from a visit. There was something very strange
about it. She should have been having some sort of reaction.

After a few minutes of rehashing the scene at the hospital, I
left Bruce with the social worker and went up to join the girls. I
could hear the soft sounds of the girls' voices as I went upstairs.
I couldn't make out the words, only a tone that suggested one
child in distress and another comforting. I hesitated at the top of

the stairs, not wanting to interrupt but dreadfully curious about what Daisy was saying.

The door to the little's room stood slightly ajar. I knocked softly before pushing it open. "Hey, girls. Mind if I come in?"

Daisy sat hunched on her bed. Karen nestled by her side with an arm draped protectively across Daisy's shoulder. They stopped talking when I came in but remained sitting as they were, just holding and being held. People wonder, I know. They think I must be crazy to choose to spend my days with kids like these: kids who smell bad and eat with their hands and tell us things we would rather not know. I wonder myself sometimes. On the days when the children fuss all day and the laundry piles up and I don't speak to a single person over three feet tall, I ponder my life and think about the ease of a classroom, where three o'clock and June always arrive. But I have moments like this, too, and then I remember why I'm here.

We spent the rest of the day getting organized. Until Jamal and Lorrell left for good, I was over my allowed number of kids. Since neither Angie nor Neddy was eighteen yet, officially, they were counted toward the number of children living at home. I could get a waiver because Daisy had been with us before. But it required jumping through some hoops and having a social worker visit every week until my numbers came down. I didn't mind: I actually enjoyed the time spent with my own social worker, Susan. But I knew that she had better things to do with her time than assure a bunch of administrators who had never met me that I wasn't overwhelmed.

Evenings at my house are orchestrated chaos. Dinner, followed by dishes, followed by assembly-line baths and pajamas. Teeth are brushed and stories read, then it's bedtime with the assorted delay tactics and tuck-ins. I can count on at least one crisis. Some, like lost teddy bears, are easily remedied. Others are not so simple.

I put Jamal to bed first. For all of his activity during the day, he crashed at night. Maggie was in next. She too usually went down well, although she was often up three or four times during the night. Karen was hard to settle. Her tics had escalated to the point that lying still was almost impossible, and she was plagued by intrusive thoughts and obsessions. I ached for her, but there wasn't much I could do beyond a fairly complicated nighttime ritual of relaxation exercises and soothing music. Lorrell was still tiny and on her own schedule. She usually slept from eight until eleven o'clock. On Daisy's first night I left Bruce to see to Karen and Maggie so we could have some private time. Daisy needed to process what must have been an excruciating day. For that matter, so did I. Sometimes things move so quickly for foster parents. It is easy to lose sight of the very real fact that we are traumatized by our children's lives, too. It is impossible for anybody with any imagination to avoid absorbing some of the pain and confusion the kids we care about are experiencing.

It was late summer and still warm enough to sit on the deck, although the chill in the evening air reminded me that fall was approaching. The faintest tinge of red was on the sugar maples, and our resident cardinal had made her first appearance at our feeders since April. I brought my evening coffee outside and called Daisy to join me. She was dressed in a long cotton nightgown that emphasized her leanness. I thought it possible she had lost weight.

"You look cold, Daisy. Come and wrap up with me." I pulled her into my lap and wrapped us both in an old afghan. She wiggled her bony frame into the hollow of my arms. I dropped my face and inhaled the sweet smell of little girl and baby shampoo.

"Pretty rough day, huh, Daisy? Do you want to talk about it?"

"My mommy got very, very mad at me. She yelled at me and called the peoples to take me away."

"Any idea why she was so mad?"

"Cause I hitted her with my slipper."

"You must have been pretty mad. What do you think made you so mad at your mom?"

The pause that followed my question was so long that I thought Daisy was not going to answer. Then she took a deep breath.

"He hurted me, you know. He hurted me every day, and she never told him to stop. He even hurted Rickey and me together, and she didn't stop him. Rickey was only a baby. Why didn't she never come when I called her?"

My mind was spinning with this talk. I assumed Daisy was talking about her mom's old boyfriend, Frank, but the name Rickey was a new one to me.

"Honey, I don't know who you're talking about. Who's Rickey?"

"He's the baby Frank brings. He makes us play Mommy and Daddy, and then he plays Mommy and Daddy with us. I call my mommy, but she's too busy and she don't never come."

I was fighting a very real urge to vomit. "Your mommy was home when Frank hurt you?"

"I think she home." Daisy didn't sound sure about that.

"Daisy. This is very important. Who did Rickey belong to? He must have had a mommy and daddy."

"I didn't see anybody with him. Just Frank."

"It must have made you pretty mad when that was happening, Daisy. I would have been mad if somebody was hurting me and my mom didn't come to save me. I bet I would have felt like hitting her, too. But I think you may be wrong about this. I think your mom didn't know what Frank was doing. I think maybe you wished she knew, but she didn't. As soon as she knew, she made him leave. And she sent you here so you would be safe."

"Please, God," I prayed silently, "let me be right about that. Let it be true that she really didn't know."

Daisy and I talked for a while longer. She gave me details I didn't want to know. There is very little a kid can tell me that I haven't heard before, but an adult forcing babies to engage in sex was outside the pale, even for me. It took every ounce of self-control I could muster to listen and respond without letting the disgust I felt come through.

I slept that night, although not well and not before I spent a good long time talking with Bruce about everything that had happened.

The next few days flew by in the kind of contained hurricane that so often seemed to define my life. Evelyn came back to work on Monday and was filled in on the events of the previous week, although not by me. Evelyn was so mad, furious, in fact, that

Glenna had not been able to manage Daisy at home that she refused to take Daisy into care on another voluntary placement.
Evelyn filed a care and protection petition in court, and Daisy
became an official ward of the state, complete with an attorney
and a service plan that allowed only supervised visitations with
Glenna.

I talked to Toni Tonelli several times during the next week,
and she saw Daisy twice. Toni was the only person besides me to
whom Daisy confided the details of her sexual abuse. Daisy was
assigned the same attorney who had represented Karen before
her adoption. Sam Zdarski was an excellent attorney, who was
dedicated to his clients. I wasn't surprised that he came out to
visit Daisy within a week of being assigned her case. He didn't
ask her a lot of questions; he concentrated on letting her get
comfortable with him. He did spend a good deal of time talking
to me about the history of her placement, what we thought
about her mother, and what our commitment to her was. I knew
where all this was leading to.

"She's an odd little duck, isn't she?"

I laughed at Sam's assessment of Daisy. "She's a little odd,
but she's a sweetheart, Sam. Not a mean bone in her body. I can't
imagine her hurting anybody, especially her mom, but I've seen
her in action over there. She walks in the door, and it's like she
flips a switch. She's climbing on the counters and screaming at
Glenna. You wouldn't believe she was the same kid."

"What does the therapist think?"

"She isn't sure. Maybe it's a kind of posttraumatic reaction
from being back in the house where the abuse took place, or it

could be that she holds her mother responsible for what happened."

"This Frank is a real piece of work, isn't he?"

"What's going to happen with that, Sam? Daisy hasn't disclosed to anybody but Toni and me. Can he be indicted if she won't talk to the DA?"

"There isn't any point in pursuing an indictment if Daisy can't testify. Even if she manages to tell a nice lady in an office somewhere, what are the chances she can still pull it off in a courtroom full of strangers, with Frank sitting there staring at her? I'm afraid old Frank is very likely to walk on this one."

"It's not right, Sam!" I fumed. "A kid gets raped by some sleazebag excuse for a human being, and then the court rapes her again, only this time in public. There is no way that fragile little thing can tell about having intercourse with a baby on the witness stand, and everybody knows it. So old Frank is free to do it again to some other little kids. As far as I'm concerned, we are all guilty of abuse for what we let happen to kids."

Sam let me rant for a bit, then he broke in.

"Look, it stinks, but it's the way it is. The important thing here is what's next for Daisy. You seem pretty fond of her. How does Bruce feel about her?"

"We love her, Sam. Both of us. If Daisy needs a family, she's got one. I haven't talked to Glenna about this, but I think she may be willing to let us do a guardianship. Daisy can keep her own last name and Glenna can have as much visitation time as she wants. But this kid needs to settle someplace soon. Why do you ask? Do you think this will go to adoption?"

"I do, actually. I spoke to Glenna for quite a while this morning. Did you know she's been hospitalized for some serious depression on several occasions?" I shook my head. Sam went on. "She doesn't feel that she can handle Daisy, and her mother isn't volunteering. I think the department won't have a choice. They can't keep a kid in care forever, and there's the added question of neglect. Nobody can figure out how Frank abused this kid for so long without Glenna having a clue."

"I'm not about to start judging Glenna, Sam. I think each of us goes into parenting with a fantasy about what it's going to be like. Nobody thinks their kid is going to be odd. Nobody expects their boyfriend to molest their kid. Most people rise to the occasion and take care of their child. Not everybody can. I'm not sure that makes you a bad person."

"A lot of people would disagree with you on that one, Kathy."

"A lot of people aren't signing up to raise kids like Daisy. Until they do, they can't know anything about it. Bruce and I can speak only for ourselves. As soon as the goal for Daisy officially changes to adoption and she gets a worker, we'll submit a legal request. We would be happy to keep Daisy."

Ten

September rolled in. I love September. I love the smell of apples and burning leaves. To me, September rather than January is the start of the new year. January is a dull month of snow and ice and low, gray skies. In the crisp new air of September, anything is possible.

Daisy fitted seamlessly back into our family. There were any number of people who never realized she had ever been away. She was back in school, back in Scouts, like all my girls, and very much our kid. She no longer went to her mom's for visits. Rather, she saw her only in the company of a social worker and never at her home. They went out for lunch or to the movies, as did other children for whom the goal of a return home seemed out of reach. The change made things easier on Glenna, I think. If there was anyone else around, Daisy rarely acted up with the same intensity she reserved for Glenna.

Maggie, Karen, and Daisy went off to school looking adorable in jumpers and matching hair ribbons. Jamal and Lorrell moved in with their family. I wished them well, but I had some concerns. Adoption means hard work under the best of circumstances and these weren't the best. I worried that Tim and Janet Washington had some unrealistic ideas about adoption. They spoke to Jamal as if he never had another family, refusing to acknowledge his loss or his longing for the family he left behind. The problems this would cause might not show up for a while, but they would show up.

Daisy went on the waiting list for an adoption worker. The lists are unpredictable. I know kids who wait for months and kids who get workers right away. It all depends on caseloads. There must have been a pile of kids who had their adoptions finalized in September, because Daisy spent only six short weeks on the waiting list before I got a call from Lauren Hightower telling me that she had just been assigned to Daisy's case. This was great news for Bruce and me because Lauren knew us well from handling Jazzy's adoption, but it was better news for Daisy. Lauren was on my elite list of workers who really understood adoption issues. I never heard her spout out any of the Pollyanna nonsense I often heard from other social workers about how the love of good parents could fix any amount of abuse or neglect. Not everybody liked Lauren; she was far too direct for many. Not being one to follow the social service party line kept her from always being popular in the office, too, but I trusted her immensely. I knew she would go to the wall for one of her kids, and that was exactly the kind of advocacy I wanted for Daisy.

"I can't believe you were assigned to Daisy," I told Lauren when she called with the news. "Maggie has been waiting a lot longer, and I haven't heard anything about her."

"You mean Miss Maggie, the case from hell? I was afraid that would be the one they gave me, and I really didn't want it."

"Why not?" I asked, genuinely puzzled. "Maggie is a great kid. She's stubborn and she has a temper, but she's doing really well."

"Did you see her psychological report?" Lauren responded. "It's grim. Elaine Waters is very good at what she does, and she says all the kids in that family have very big problems."

"Elaine Waters thinks everybody's got big problems. I don't put a lot of stock in any report from someone who's spent about four hours with a kid. How can you tell anything substantial from that? Marney Scott from the Children's Clinic has seen her. She doesn't see any of the problems that the testing showed. I have a lot of faith in Marney. She's very smart, and she knows Maggie a lot better than Elaine."

"You trust her because she agrees with you." Lauren laughed. "I'm not saying that Maggie hasn't made progress. I'm just saying that there is a lot we don't know about all of these kids. Both parents are seriously mentally ill. The feeling in the adoption unit is that it wouldn't be fair to try to find families for the kids until we have more information. I don't think they'll even get a worker until next spring. So let's get to Daisy. Rumor has it that you and Bruce want to keep her."

"Rumor is right. I think we can work with Glenna and give Daisy the best of both worlds, a stable place to grow up in and an ongoing relationship with her mother."

"I have to tell you, Kathy, I have some reservations about this adoption," countered Lauren. "I think you have a lot on your plate right now. Karen has a pretty serious diagnosis, and I don't think raising Daisy will be a walk in the park. Her psychological doesn't look very good, either."

"All the more reason to leave her here. We know the issues, and we're prepared for the future. A new family might not understand what they're getting into. I talked to Al Hamilton last week. Jazzy is giving them a terrible time. They love her, and they aren't going to give her back, but I think they find it a lot harder than they expected. She just destroyed her bedroom because they put her in time-out. We can tell families and tell them, but who would believe some sweet little cherub can knock over a dresser?"

"I'm meeting with Glenna this afternoon. I'm going to bring up the subject of doing an open adoption with you and Bruce. We'll see where it goes. I need to locate Daisy's father, too. I have no idea what his role has been in her life, but we can't proceed without figuring that piece out."

Much was going on behind the scenes while Bruce and I worked on getting Daisy settled back in. I knew Frank had been interviewed several times, although nothing came of it. He admitted to watching his sister's child, a baby boy named Rickey, from time to time while Glenna was at work, but he denied any sexual misconduct. The sister was questioned but said her little boy had a fine relationship with his uncle, although they spent little time together since the child was now in preschool. The criminal case was at a complete standstill unless Daisy opened up to someone in the DA's office.

We had mentioned nothing of adoption to Daisy, and neither did Glenna. She was still struggling with her decision, not at all sure it was the right thing for her or Daisy. She knew that Bruce and I hoped to raise Daisy. Now that Lauren was onboard to handle the supervised visitations, we rarely saw each other.

The house felt very empty. I was regularly turning down children who didn't seem right for us. The office had a run on boys, and unless they were very young, I didn't provide care to boys. They always had a glut of adolescent girls. Girls in this age group are often sexually active and have a history of drug use. Also, a disproportionate number of them seem to become involved with older men. Add to these problems the other common issues of adolescence, eating disorders and cutting, and you have a population that scares a lot of families. Unfortunately, this makes it hard for the girls who aren't in real trouble, the ones who are just looking for a safe haven so they can finish school and have some help while they try to fashion a life for themselves without family support. I often wished that I had about a million dollars to play with. I had a fantasy about the perfect home for sixteen-year-old girls. It would include supported autonomy and a strong therapeutic component. But in my real world, with three fragile little girls, two teenage daughters, and a handsome nineteen-year-old son at home, caring for teenage girls for more than a night or two seemed like a very bad idea.

We finally said yes to a set of sisters. By the time the girls had been with us for about three weeks, I thought back to the children I had not taken, the hyperactive six-year-old boy, the anorexic fifteen-year-old girl with the twenty-five-year-old boyfriend, the newborn with cerebral palsy. Each and every day, I asked myself, "What was I thinking?"

Ruth and Mary Margaret were eleven and thirteen. Their parents lived a vagabond life, skipping from state to state, always one step ahead of the social service agencies who tried to pressure the parents to provide the kids with even a modicum of basic care. Unbelievable as it may be, in a country of abundance there are children who go to bed hungry and have never seen a dentist. Ruth and Mary Margaret had no place to call home but the back of a van. Their clothes came from charity boxes. They didn't own a toothbrush. The parents justified their neglect behind a curtain of fundamental Christian values. Their religion was also their excuse for beating the girls on a pretty regular basis. The van was pulled over on the Massachusetts turnpike by a state police office who noticed that it had no inspection sticker. He took one look at the thin little girls with the bruised faces and called social services from his radio. The girls were taken to the police station and then brought to us, late on a Thursday evening.

I hear sad stories every day, but this one ripped at my heart. I couldn't wait to introduce the girls to regular meals and pretty clothes and clean sheets. One would think that after providing care to dozens of children in crisis, I would have become immune to the fantasy of happily-ever-after and oh-so-grateful for the rescued children, but I slipped this time. I watched these two emaciated children gobble down leftover meatloaf and delight in the luxury of a hot shower and a bed of their very own, and I was hooked. Who could resist? Ruth was a tiny doe-eyed thirteen-year-old who prayed before meals and referred to Bruce and me as "Sir" and "Ma'am." She liked to read Bible stories and had never heard of Britney Spears. Mary Margaret had the same impeccable manners and tiny frame, but she was blond and dimpled. They were irresistible for the better part of two weeks.

This is the part that is so difficult to fathom until you live it. You can't just pull children from a bad situation and expect them to forget. It's in them someplace, the pain and the rage and the overwhelming grief, and it will come out. Ruth began to act out first, not against Bruce or me, but against all the little girls, especially Karen. It was several weeks before she was confident enough to trust that we wouldn't hurt her and she could turn on us. I got it. I really did. Karen had, to Ruth's mind, everything. It wasn't so much the stuff that Ruth resented, although I'm sure it rankled to see the dolls and the CD player and the bike and the books that Karen was so able to take for granted. Rather, it was the easy intimacy she enjoyed with her parents and her brothers and sisters that was the cause of the worst jealousy. Ruth was old enough and sophisticated enough in the ways of psychological warfare, having so often been the target, that she was able to get to Karen in a number of really hurtful small ways. She teased her about her worries and rituals and zeroed in on her tics, making cruel remarks just loud enough to be certain that Karen heard. Ruth teased Daisy about her eating and Maggie about her pudgy tummy and wandering eye, but that was more for sport. When she wanted to draw blood, she always went after Karen.

Mary Margaret was a different sort. She turned on the charm whenever she was out in public, especially at school and at church. I was constantly approached by people who met Mary Margaret away from home who wanted to discuss her situation and whether she might need a family. I was beginning to feel like the Wal-Mart children's division, the place to go if you wanted to adopt but didn't have a lot of money. I usually appreciate legitimate inquiries about children who are on the adoption track. A lot of kids have found very good families because of their connection to a community. But any questions about Mary Margaret made me intensely uncomfortable. I knew that the face she presented in public was vastly different from the one we saw at home, one that was becoming increasingly hostile and inaccessible. She didn't scream at us the way Ruth did. Instead, after she had been spoken to, she would retreat upstairs. I wouldn't find out until hours or sometimes days later that she had been very been busy, scribbling on walls and, once, gouging deep furrows in a new bureau.

I hung in for several months, much longer than I should have. In cool retrospect, I wonder why. I fear I know the answer, but I take no pleasure in admitting it. There was a certain ego jolt I got from caring for these particular girls. They put on a good deal of weight and gained several inches in height. I spent weeks bringing their immunizations up-to-date and figuring educational plans to help them catch up in school. They wore new clothes and had bicycles. People commented on how well they looked and how much progress we had made. Foster parents get precious few pats on the back. Caring for Ruth and Mary Margaret assured me lots of pats. But they were expensive pats. Unfortunately, it was Karen and Maggie and Daisy who paid for them by losing the kind of home they had come to depend upon. One snowy afternoon Ruth attacked again. We had been arguing over the art closet. I insisted that the supplies belonged to all the children. Ruth wanted to keep the little girls out until she was finished with a project. It was over nothing. It was over everything.

"You're an evil, ugly woman. No wonder you got a tic kid. God gave her to you to punish you for being mean."

I didn't respond. I couldn't. Not without saying something that would take me to a place where I didn't want to go. I picked up the phone and called a friend who had been a foster parent for several years. I didn't give her any details. I just said I needed to find someone to take Ruth, and I couldn't wait until the office opened on Monday. Ruth had to leave now.

It is a measure of my friendship with Joanna that she didn't ask why Ruth had to leave or why I called her instead of the hotline. She simply said that her husband could be there in thirty minutes, and asked if things would be all right until then. I assured her they would, thanked her, hung up, and turned to Ruth.

"You can't hurt people like this, Ruth. You can't say whatever you like and think it won't matter, because it will. I'm sorry this didn't work out, but you can't stay here and say things that hurt my other kids. I'm sorry. I have a safe place for you to go. We'll call your social worker on Monday and find another home for you. You have about a half hour to pack. I'll bring you an overnight bag. Take just what you'll need for the rest of the weekend. I'll send the rest along to your new placement." Then I went into the bedroom and shut the door.

The wait for Philip was deadly quiet. I brought the little girls into my room and let them play dress-up. I said only that things were not going well and that Ruth would be spending the weekend with Joanna and Philip. It was harder with Mary Margaret. She was such a closed, insular little girl. She displayed not a sign of grief or the smallest hint of anger. I worried about what simmered beneath that cool, solemn exterior. I feared it was something dark and scary. I knew I didn't want to be in the way when it finally revealed itself. Getting Mary Margaret to talk was impossible, at least for me. She turned on the television and sat alone in the living room watching a football game.

I learned something valuable with Ruth. It is a large truth and an important one for those charged with the care of children who are not easy to care for. Child abuse is an insidious thing. It doesn't always barge through the front door of your home and announce its presence. Sometimes it creeps in quietly, takes a

seat, and acts as though it belongs. I could have hurt Ruth. I
didn't. But I peeked through the door for a moment, surprised
to find that it was in my house, too.

Joanna and Philip kept Ruth for nearly three weeks. Then
she began the bounce. A month with one family, a weekend with
another. Ruth was a little girl in big trouble. I kept up with her
whereabouts because of Mary Margaret. Not that she asked
about her sister. She didn't. Nor did she ask about her parents,
both of whom were in jail on a number of charges. I wondered if
she cared at all or if all the caring had been beaten out of her a
long time ago.

Mary Margaret was drifting at our house, with us but not a
part of us. She never asked for anything and wouldn't or couldn't
accept so much as a hug. When I got a call from her social worker
in the week following Christmas, telling me that an adoptive
placement had been found, I was torn. I was glad she was leaving. This had been the most unrewarding child I had ever cared
for. But I felt for the family that was adopting her. I knew the
movie that played for them in the minutes before sleep found
them. They envisioned Mary Margaret running up to them with
her arms outstretched. They could hear her calling for them.
They saw their daughters sharing secrets and laughing together
on the couch. Life as a Hallmark moment.

I met with Andrew and Alice Riley twice before Mary Margaret moved in with them. No one saw any reason for a longer
transition since she had no connection to us. The first time we
met, I told them what we knew of this child. She was distant and
cool. She didn't have tantrums, but it would behoove them to

keep an eye on her if she was angry. She was bright. She was healthy. She read the Bible a lot. The second time I spoke to them was the day before the move. They called to ask what she might need. Did she have enough winter clothes and a sled? Would they need to buy her skates? I knew the real reason for the call had little to do with coats or skates. They were expectant, expecting, in the real sense of the word, and they wanted to share their excitement with someone. I wanted to tell them to run, run like the wind, because I thought this child had the potential to break their hearts. These were nice people, and they deserved a kid who could love them. I didn't believe Mary Margaret was that kid. I felt as though I were throwing them to the wolves.

Mary Margaret left the next morning. Neither Karen, Maggie, nor Daisy came downstairs to see her off. I carried her things out to the car and turned to give her a hug good-bye, but she was already gone. I could see her silhouette in the car window. Alice looked a bit embarrassed.

"It must be too difficult for her to say good-bye to you. She's been here so long—this must be so painful for all of you."

What the heck was I supposed to say to that?

Eleven

I didn't realize how much my energy had been drained by caring for Ruth and Mary Margaret until both girls were gone and I began to recover. I took a three-year-old child who spoke very little English, which I guess made us even because I spoke very little Spanish. Lupe was obviously brighter than I was because I gave up on mastering any more than the fundamentals of her language, whereas she quickly became totally fluent in mine. She was exactly the child we needed just then. She was an imp, into everything and in constant motion. After a long day of chasing Lupe, I would collapse on the sofa, laughing with Bruce over her antics and looking forward to the next day. Then we took a baby girl, Lakita, who likely had fetal alcohol syndrome. This meant that the whole round of specialists from early intervention services was coming by each week. Once again my days were packed, and I couldn't have been happier.

Well, I could have been. Every time Karen developed a new tic, my heart broke again. And the tics were coming fast and furious. Her head jerked back so often that she had a constant cramp in her neck. She had tics in her fingers and in her toes. She hummed and cleared her throat and made an odd little *phhhht* sound. We were learning what made the tics worse. Stress certainly did. So did too much noise and too much activity. Karen needed enough sleep, regular meals, and a lot of exercise. We were also learning that although a lot of things made them worse, there wasn't much that made them better once they started. There were medications that would help, but when Bruce and I read about the side effects, things like cognitive dulling, weight gain, and hand tremors, we dismissed the treatment as being far worse than the disease.

Unfortunately, Tourette's syndrome is rarely a lone intruder in a child's life. It travels in tandem with some other disorders. The majority of people who are diagnosed with Tourette's also have obsessive-compulsive disorder. As Karen turned six, she developed a serious problem with OCD. She was compelled to count every window, every ceiling tile, every book in a room, over and over, never sure she had it quite right. She washed her hands until they were red and raw and became so convinced that something would happen to me while she was away that she was unable to go to school. We received help from an outstanding therapist and an amazing psychiatrist, both affiliated with the Children's Clinic. With their guidance we were able to help Karen manage her more troubling symptoms, but both doctors were clear with us. Karen was severely affected with both Tourette's and OCD. Things were going to become a lot worse for her before there was any hope of their getting better.

With all Karen was going through, the question had to be asked: What were we thinking? How could we even consider adding another child, number seven no less, to the family? Especially a child like Daisy. I wasn't naive enough to expect that she would go through life without paying the emotional price for the damage done to her by Frank. Sexual abuse is a terrible thing to happen to child. It is far worse than a beating. It brings with it shame as well as violation, and I know of few children able to believe they are not somehow at fault. To be used sexually by the person you trust to care for you wounds a child's soul. The pain is further compounded when the perpetrator doesn't have to answer for his crimes. I don't mean in the criminal sense. I have not had many children who wished to see their parent in jail. What they want is an apology, some acknowledgment that what was done to them was wrong and that the adult is sorry for the harm done.

Why did I want Daisy? The only answer I could come up with then and still believe today is that life presents itself to us. There are these amazing opportunities to love and we have to grab them. Life with all of my children was sometimes very, very hard, but here is the truth I hope to teach them: We don't get to make choices about what is handed to us. Our only choice is in the way we react. I expected Karen and Daisy to do well, not because they had easy lives. They didn't. They were both challenged more by the time they were seven than I was likely to be in my whole life. I expected them to do well because it was their nature to find joy and love in the most unlikely places. I couldn't protect them, but I could hold their hands through the hard times that were sure to come their way.

Believing this, I wanted to get Daisy settled. I was hearing very little from Lauren. She picked Daisy up for visits, but we didn't talk much. I was hearing nothing from Glenna. Sam came by each month, but he too was more quiet than I remember him being when he was coming to see Karen. I attributed that to the fact that Karen had been a baby, and Sam had no choice but to talk to me about her. Daisy was a little girl, and his job was to speak for her. To do that, he had to know what she wanted. That meant that he had to spend enough time with her so that he could not only advise her but hear what she thought about her life and her future.

That was a subject I wouldn't have been much help with because I had no idea what Daisy wanted to happen to her. She was a child who lived completely in the present. I was used to having children always questioning. "When is the next visit? How many days till my birthday? When am I going home? Are we there yet? How come I have to live with you?" Daisy never asked questions like that. It made a good deal of her life a delightful surprise, but it didn't provide the opening I needed to talk with her about adoption.

Toni wasn't talking to her about adoption in therapy, either. There were bigger things to work on there. I didn't attend sessions with Daisy, although I did transport her every week. I was struck by how she changed when we entered the clinic. The bubbly, happy, if somewhat goofy kid we all saw at home was transformed into a morose, teary little waif. She would huddle in the corner of the sofa in the waiting room, wrapped up in an old sweater that Toni left for her. Her eyes glazed over and she reverted to a whimpering baby talk I heard nowhere else. She sucked ferociously on her thumb. It was tempting to think that this was all an enormous bid for attention or sympathy, but that was just not Daisy's style. I think it more likely that she was remarkably perceptive. She recognized the value of the clinic. In this place as in no other, Daisy was free to do the work she needed to do. It was plodding and painful, but she never complained about going. I could hear her heavy steps treading up the stairs, and she disappeared for nearly an hour, then returned with the same leaden walk. Recovery was slow. It often took hours after a session for Daisy to return to normal. Unlike so many other children, Daisy never shared what went on once she went upstairs. I didn't think it wise to press her. Therapy belonged very much to Toni and Daisy. I had no place there.

The holidays approached. We found that many children are overwhelmed by the too-muchness of Christmas, so we kept our own celebration low-key and simple. We baked cookies and decorated a large tree. Our tree was always bottom heavy because the children couldn't reach very high, and it was laden with handmade ornaments, glittery pinecones, sequined baubles, and multicolored God's eyes. We went to church on Christmas Eve and took a tour of the surrounding hills to seek the best outdoor displays. Other than that, we stayed home. We built snow dragons and consumed far more hot chocolate than was good for anybody. But we had fun, and the kids didn't seem to notice that it was far from the elaborate celebrations of some of their friends. Having a television but no reception was helpful. Since my kids didn't see anything advertised, they never begged for anything. It made for a very pleasant time.

January was a deceptively mild month. I might well have believed that we were headed for a warm and early spring had I not lived through spells like this before. They never last, at least not in New England, and they are usually followed by icy rains and limb-snapping winds. By February it was clear that the mild weather had been a tease and that winter was far from over. The girls were stuck inside for days at a time and beginning to get on one another's nerves. They were tired of the same old games and stale activities. In desperation, I got a sitter for the baby on the first Tuesday of the February break and planned a trip to a huge local greenhouse, where we could wander through the humid tropical air and dream of spring. The girls were dressed and the snacks packed when the phone rang. I nearly left it for the sitter to deal with, but I had older kids on the road. I knew myself well enough to know that I would worry all afternoon if I didn't take the call.

"Hi, Kathy. It's Lauren. I feel like it's been months since we've talked. How is my little friend doing?"

"She's doing great, Lauren, but we're just on our way out the door. Do you need something or can I call you back when I get home?"

"I need to drop by. I haven't seen Daisy yet this month, and I need to talk to you about something. Are you going to be around tomorrow?"

"I am, but all the kids are home on break. I don't mind if you don't mind, but you won't have any privacy."

"I was thinking I might take Daisy out actually, but I need to talk to you, too. Is one o'clock okay?"

"That's fine. I might even have a couple in for naps."

We said our good-byes, and I headed out with the girls. It was a lovely afternoon. The greenhouse was affiliated with a local university. It was fascinating. There was an alien quality to the air; I wouldn't have been surprised to see a python resting on the limb of a banana tree or a tiger resting underneath. The exotic blooms and heady fragrances were the perfect antidote to the February blahs.

I spent the next morning in the kitchen getting ready for Lauren's visit. I knew I didn't really have to go to a lot of trouble. It wasn't likely that she would see dirty dishes in the sink or realize that I sometimes gave the kids cold cereal for breakfast and decide that I was unfit to adopt, but that didn't matter to the crazed woman I was capable of becoming. The house was cleaned and the girls freshly bathed. Lauren was greeted with home-made cookies and a pot of good tea.

Daisy was all over Lauren. It is typical for children in foster care to latch on to their social workers. I think these children must often feel as though they live on the fringes of a family, even in a home like ours, where the extended family went out of their way to make the kids feel included and part of the group. Both sets of grandparents were very welcoming and never brought a gift for one child without bringing a gift for all of the children. Even so, the kids looked forward to visits from their social workers. It was one of the few times they felt singled out in a special way. It was odd but, even when the worker was delivering bad news, few younger kids held the worker responsible for it. It was more likely they would ultimately blame me. I was the mother, and I was supposed to be able to fix everything.

"Hey, Daisy," I interrupted her, as she went on and on about our trip to the greenhouse. "Why don't you save the rest of that story for your visit with Lauren? I hear she's taking you out later."

"Just one more thing. Okay? I just tell her about one more thing and then I stop."

I had to laugh. Daisy's "one more thing" could go on for fifteen minutes. Since her return to us, she had changed in a subtle but very nice way. Daisy was more open. She was more mischievous too and less worried that she might do something wrong. On occasion, I even had to reprimand her slightly. I didn't do it often, and I was always gentle because she was still a sensitive little girl and easily wounded by words one of the other kids would have brushed off. But I knew Lauren's time was limited and I really needed to talk to her.

"Not now, Daisy. You can tell Lauren all about it later. Now scoot upstairs with the other kids."

Daisy scooted, albeit reluctantly, and Lauren and I settled on the sofa.

"I recognize that look, Lauren. What's up? I'm thinking it's nothing good."

"You know me pretty well, Kathy. It's not good. I located Daisy's father. He lives in Pennsylvania. He's married. He's got a couple of other kids. And he wants Daisy."

"Just like that. He wants Daisy. That's crazy, right? I mean, you aren't considering it, are you?"

Lauren's silence was her only answer.

My sudden anger surprised me. "Well, where the hell has Daddy Dearest been the past year and a half? Where was he while I was feeding his kid through a straw? Where was he when some pervert was hurting her? How many times did I paste her back together after a visit or after therapy?" I struggled to keep my voice down, but it was breaking and I fought back tears.

"I don't blame you, Kathy, but I need you to listen to me. This guy is not a monster. When he and Glenna broke up, Daisy was just a baby. He thought it would be better for Daisy if he just dropped quietly out of her life. He and Glenna's mother didn't get along at all, and his breakup with Glenna was pretty unpleasant. He didn't want Daisy stuck in the middle of a bunch of warring adults. It made sense to him at the time, and he certainly had no way of knowing about Frank. Now that he knows, he wants his daughter. His record is clean. He has a good job and a stable marriage. Legally, we can't stop him from taking Daisy, and I'm not sure we should, even if we could."

"How can you say that, Lauren?" I said angrily. "You're the one who's always talking about how important connections are for kids. Daisy is attached to us. She thinks of us as her family. She doesn't even know this guy."

"She's attached to you, and she can attach to her father. I know this is hard. . . ."

"You don't know anything. You walk in here and tell me this, and then you go home. This is my life, Lauren. This isn't just some kid. This is Daisy. How am I just supposed to let her go like she doesn't matter? Like she's just a placement, and we're nothing but a bed. Look. What would our chances be if we wanted to go to court on this? What if we got a lawyer and fought this?"

"You would be wasting your money and hurting Daisy. And you wouldn't have the support of the department. Please don't make this any more difficult than it needs to be. Daisy has a dad who wants her. You don't have a choice."

Lauren continued to talk, but I was in no condition to listen to reason. After a few minutes, she picked up her coat and called Daisy downstairs.

Daisy left with Lauren, and they were gone for the rest of the day. By late afternoon I was getting paranoid. I had visions of Lauren taking Daisy back to the office and looking for another foster home for her. Of course she didn't do that. She returned at five with Daisy—a spinning, flapping, almost incoherent Daisy.

I sat on the sofa and pulled Daisy into my arms. "Slow down, kiddo. I can't understand you when you talk so fast."

"I got a father. A real father. Not like Frank. Like Bruce. And he comin to see me and he buyed me a doll. I got a sister and a brother not pretend but real, and they comin too and a stepped-on mother, but I didn't never see them and . . ."

"Okay, Daisy, slow down. This is a lot of exciting news all at once. Let's talk about one thing at a time. I think that will be easier. Tell me about your dad. What's his name?"

Daisy looked as if she was going to cry. "He's got a name?" She sounded panicked. "I thought I could call him Daddy. I don't know his name."

"Of course you can call him Daddy, Daisy. But he has another name. Like Bruce. Karen calls him Daddy, but I call him Bruce. I'm Mommy and Kathy. I wondered what your dad's other name is."

Lauren answered for Daisy. "His name is Evan. Daisy saw a picture of him today. He's very tall, isn't he, Daisy?"

"My mom showed me a picture of him holding me when I was a little baby."

"I didn't know you were going to Glenna's." Already I felt as if I was losing Daisy. As if I was a little out of the loop.

Lauren must have caught the tone in my voice. "I thought it would be a good idea for Glenna to tell Daisy what is going to be happening. I wanted Daisy to know that her mom thinks it's a good idea for her to live with her dad."

I felt terrible for Bruce. I had tried to reach him all day to fill him in about what was going on, but he had been out of his office. I had all afternoon to process the news about a father for Daisy, but Bruce was hit with it the minute he walked in the door. Plus, no sooner had he taken off his jacket than Daisy arrived, and he had to act as if it were good news, as if we were happy about it.

"So your dad is coming this weekend, Daisy. That's exciting." Bruce's voiced sounded strained. I knew he was struggling to keep his tone even.

"That was the soonest we could get everything worked out," answered Lauren. "He's driving up with his family. They still have friends in the area they can stay with. They would like to come to see Daisy on Saturday. I know it's short notice, but I didn't think you would mind." There was a question in Lauren's voice that had nothing to do with the inconvenience of an unexpected visit.

"Of course we don't mind. Will they want her on Sunday, too?"

"They sure would. In fact, they'll be here for a whole week, and they want to spend as much time as they can with Daisy." Lauren's voice was hearty. "Daisy and her family have a lot of catching up to do. They need to get to know one another if Daisy is going to be living with them."

Daisy remained locked in my arms while we talked. She felt wooden, as though she was struggling to keep herself together. I recognized the look on Daisy's face. It might have been mistaken for excitement by someone who didn't know her as well as I did, but it was the panic that went along with a loss of control. This was too much to ask of anybody. A new life handed to you as though it was a gift, and Daisy was supposed to be what—grateful? I could imagine what she must be feeling. I had heard it from kids too many times. Who asked for this gift? Not Daisy, certainly. Not many of the kids who found themselves on the receiving end of society's generosity.

Lauren stayed for a while longer. In spite of my earlier tirade, I knew Lauren trusted me to do the right thing for Daisy. She was right to trust me. I might be hurting, but I wouldn't say or do anything that would make this move harder on Daisy. I might hate it, but I would be a grown-up.

We fed the kids, bathed them, and got them ready for bed. Karen had a hard time settling down. "But I don't want Daisy to leave, Mama," she cried over and over. "I like Daisy. She's my best friend. Who am I going to play with?"

I knew there was another unspoken question behind her distress. "If Daisy can leave, how can I know I'm safe? How can I know someone won't show up to claim me someday, too?" It was a legitimate worry. Karen had seen us let go of children we claimed to love every day.

"I want you to listen to me, Karen. You are our very precious daughter. Daddy and I love you more than anything in the whole wide world."

"Bigger than the moon?"

"Bigger than the moon."

"Bigger than the sun?"

"Way bigger than the sun."

"Bigger than the whole universe?"

"Even bigger than that."

"All the way up to God?"

"All the way up to God. Adoption means forever, and we would never, ever let you go."

"What if my other daddy from before came to get me? What would you do?"

"Daddy and I would get very ferocious. Young Bruce and Nathan and Ben and Angie and Neddy and Daddy and I would stand in a circle around you, and we would not let him take you. 'This is our little girl and you can't have her' is what we would say in our fiercest voices, and he would have to go away."

"Daddy is very strong, isn't he?"

"He's the strongest daddy I know, Button. He will always keep you safe."

When Karen finally settled down, I went in to Daisy. Bruce was already there, talking softly to her in the dark of the room. He looked silly, with his tall frame hunched up on her little bed, but he looked sweet, too. He was good at this stuff with the kids, better than I am in a lot of ways. He was more inclined to listen and less inclined to think he had to fix everything.

"Is this a private conversation, or can I join you?"

"We were hoping you would come in. Daisy has a lot of questions, and I don't have a lot of answers. She wants to know why she is going to live with her dad instead of her mom. She wonders if it is because she was a bad girl and hit her mom. What do you think? Do you think Daisy has to live with her dad because she's a bad girl?"

"This is a grown-up decision. It doesn't have anything to do with how you behave, Daisy. Your mom loves you, but she can't figure out how to help you when you have a hard time. She'll always be your mom, but it may not be a good idea for you to live together. Lots of people love each other but don't live together."

"Are we getting a divorce?"

"No, sweetie. Kids don't get divorced from their parents. Your mom will always be your mom, no matter where you live."

This was beginning to sound plastic to me. I had said the words too often and to too many kids. Daisy deserved better than that from me.

"Here it is, Daisy. This stinks. I wish you didn't have to go. I know your mom wishes she could keep you closer to her. But your dad doesn't live here. He lives in Pennsylvania, and that's where you will live, too. Tomorrow I'll show you on a map where that is. It is pretty far away but not so far that you won't be able to come back and visit sometimes."

"What if I don't want to go?"

"You have to go, Daisy. It's where your family is. It's where you belong."

Her face was turned from me, and I could barely make out her final words.

"Belong should be up to the person, I think. Belong should be the place where you're happy."

The next few days whirled past me. Daisy's lawyer, Sam, came by to talk with Daisy before we went into court for the custody hearing. He tried to have a conversation with her, but she was too anxious to pull it off. He finally took pity on her and sent her off to play with Karen. I was grateful to have a chance to speak with him privately.

"Sam, there has to be a way to stop this move. You've seen Daisy. Does she look like a kid who wants this to happen?"

"My job is to represent what my client wants to the judge unless my client isn't old enough or isn't capable of making an informed decision. I know Daisy would probably say she wanted to stay here, if I asked her that. The problem is in her capacity to make an informed decision. I don't think she can. I have to speak to what's in her best interest, and I think that's to go to her father's."

"How do you figure that? He hasn't cared enough to even visit with her. Now he wants to raise her. I think the department is just happy to get rid of a messy case, and this is the easy way out."

"I want you to understand something," Sam answered. "I am not trying to take the easy way out on this case. I've spent hours on the phone. I've talked to Evan and his wife. I talked to his kids' teachers and his supervisor at work. I spent a good hour on the phone with Evan's parish priest. This is not a bad guy, Kathy. I wouldn't be supporting this move if I weren't sure it was going to be good for Daisy."

After talking to Sam, I began the process of accepting the inevitable. Daisy was moving, and I couldn't stop it. I could cooperate and make it as easy on all of us as I could or I could fight it and make everyone miserable in the process. I set up a meeting with Toni Tonelli to discuss how to do this thing. We got through the hour by concentrating on the basics of what might help and on the concrete stuff of a move. Daisy would need to find a new therapist and transfer her educational plan to her new school district. There was the considerable problem of transferring her health insurance so there wouldn't be a gap in services at the time she was the most vulnerable. I was good at this kind of thing, the housekeeping issues of moving. I was less good at the emotional piece. It was a point of honor to me that I not let on how tough this was for me or how much I didn't want it to happen. I did pretty well, too. At least until it came time to leave. Toni walked me to the door of the office. She leaned her head against the jamb and stood for a few seconds with her eyes closed.

"I suppose that all we can do is all we can do. Then we move on to the next kid, and we do it again." She said this quietly. I knew it was intended for both of us. "Will you call me if you need to talk?"

I started to protest that Toni had better things to do with her time than babysit me, but I thought better of it. "I'd like that, Toni. I would like to talk sometime when this is over." That was it for me. I began to weep. Toni cried with me. Neither of us had a tissue, so we stood there, two grown women, wiping our runny noses on the sleeves of our shirts and sniffling our good-byes.

With Daisy's new home ten hours away, there could be no gentle transition. Her father was staying for a week to clean up the legal issues involved in gaining sole physical custody of Daisy. He and his family would spend every minute they could with her, then return to Pennsylvania the following weekend.

Throughout the next busy days, my phone rang steadily with calls from people who needed to discuss Daisy. I heard from her teacher and from her special education consultant. I heard from her doctor and from the district attorney's office. The one person who did not call was Glenna. At first I was annoyed, until it occurred to me that she might not know what to say to me or, more to the point, what I might say to her.

It would have been so easy to let it go. Glenna could just drift from my life as had so many other mothers over the years. But it felt unfinished somehow. I owed both of us some sense of resolution.

"Hi, Glenna," I said, when I reached her some minutes later. "It's Kathy. Do you have a couple of minutes? I was hoping we could talk."

Glenna sound nervous. "I guess so. But I don't have a lot of time."

"This won't take long. It just seems this was all so sudden. I don't feel like it's really sunk in yet. How are you feeling about it? Does this seem like a good thing to you?"

"I know you won't understand, but I do think it's good." Glenna hesitated a minute. "You like it, don't you?"

"Like what?"

"All the mothering stuff. When I've been there and the kids are all crying and hanging on you and you can't finish a sentence without somebody needing something from you, you don't mind it. I can tell. Well, I hate it. I love my kid, but I'm not good at it. When Daisy was little and she'd be screaming, I couldn't stand it. Sometimes I'd have to go to my room just to get away from her for a while. When she first went into foster care, I didn't even miss her much. I was just relieved to have it over, that all the time needing me, hanging on me, blaming me because of Frank. I know she thinks I knew what he was doing to her, but I didn't. Evan is a good guy. He's boring, but he's probably a great father. I'll bet he's a scout leader and a baseball coach and president of the PTA. I can't explain it, but I just hate all of it. It's better if Daisy is with him."

I didn't know what to say to Glenna. We were certainly different people. I was very good at feeling empathy for the parents I knew who battled mental illness or substance abuse or domestic violence or poverty. I could feel what it must be like to be them. I could imagine coming from that very different place. But I could not quite get to where Glenna was, although I knew the feeling. It's easy to become overwhelmed by the needs of little children. I too had locked myself in my bedroom from time to time just to escape and remember who I was. The difference was that I always emerged. I was always happy to come back out.

"I suppose you're right. I don't think about it much, but I do like it. I can't imagine doing anything else. That doesn't mean that you have to feel the same. In your own way, you're doing as much for Daisy as I ever did. You're making sure she's getting what she needs, even though it means letting her go. I'm not sure I could manage that.

"Will you keep in touch?" I asked Glenna. "I would like to know how Daisy is doing."

Glenna paused a moment. "Probably not. I could tell you I will, but we both know I won't, so why bother."

"I know, but I wanted to ask anyway. If she ever asks about me, you can tell Daisy that I cared, that we all loved her."

"If she asks, I'll tell her. I suppose I should thank you. I never said that. I did appreciate what you did."

"You didn't have to say it, Glenna. I always knew. So did Daisy."

As if to test me, the children gave me a tough week. They were, as most children who live in foster care are, acutely aware of the mood of their caregivers. The strain that Bruce and I were living under did not go unnoticed, and they reacted accordingly. It was a week of bad dreams and wet beds, of temper tantrums and upset tummies. Saturday came, and with it spilled milk and fights over toys. Karen was teary and clingy. The baby howled every time I put her down. By the time I heard Evan's car in the drive, my nerves were frazzled. Bruce went out to greet him. I was grateful that he had come alone with Lauren. The addition of a stepmother and two siblings might have pushed us all over the edge.

Daisy disappeared as soon as she heard the car. Where she hid, I couldn't guess, but it gave me a chance to check out Evan while he, Bruce, and Lauren spoke in the yard. I had seen only one picture of him, holding Daisy. In it, he was looking down at his daughter. I couldn't really see his face. I certainly wouldn't have recognized him.

He was tall, and dark like Daisy. I was surprised that he seemed so much older than Glenna, nearly middle-aged and quite slender. Bruce led the trio into the house and performed the introductions.

Evan put out his hand shyly. I was startled by how much he looked like Daisy.

"Lauren and Toni have both told me how much you have done for Daisy. I'm so sorry it fell to you, but I'm really grateful you were there."

I could see behind Evan to the doorway that led to the hall. Daisy was crouching there, nearly out of sight.

"Hey, Daisy. There's someone out here who's come an awfully long way to see you. Don't you think you should come out here and say hello?"

Before disappearing, Daisy had been dressed in typical weekend wear, a pair of jeans and a new shirt, but that clearly had not met with Daisy's standards for special apparel. She was now wearing last spring's Easter dress. Unfortunately, she wore it backward. The dress was a sunshine yellow. It clashed with the purple tights she chose to wear, and even more with the red-and-green-plaid hair ribbon. For Daisy, though, it was an ensemble to die for.

An awkward silence plagued all of us, but Lauren came to the rescue.

"This is your dad, Daisy. He has been waiting and waiting to see you. He sounded just like one of my kids. 'Are we there yet? How many more minutes?' Come on in and sit down. I want you all to see what Evan brought with him." Lauren held out a large photograph album. "Wait until you see this. You remember I told you about your stepmother, Helen. Well, she's quite the artist and she put this together for you. It's an album filled with pictures of all the places and the people from Pennsylvania. There are pictures of your new school and the therapist who will be seeing you. You know you have a little sister. She's so excited because she's been wanting bunk beds, and now she can have them because you two will be sharing a bedroom."

While Lauren talked, she pulled Daisy between her and Evan on the sofa. It was an easy matter for him to take over and begin to tell Daisy about the pictures. In minutes, he had her laughing about their cat, who hated to hear anyone sing "Happy

Birthday," and their hamster, who escaped from his habitat on the day the priest came to visit and hid in his hat.

I was prepared not to like Evan, but he certainly didn't make it easy. He was warm and funny and so nervous that his hands trembled. After a bit Bruce and I excused ourselves. Evan, Lauren, and Daisy left to meet the rest of her family for lunch.

Daisy returned after supper, wearing a new dress and an ear-to-ear grin.

"Don't you love my dress, Kathy? My sister, Lydia, has one just like it. She's very nice. I got a brother, too, only Lydia says he's pest, but I don't got another brother so I don't care."

"I love your dress, Daisy. It's just beautiful. Maybe you could wear it for your good-bye party at school."

Evan stood shyly in the doorway. "We'll pick you up for mass in the morning, Daisy. Is nine o'clock too early?"

"Nine is fine," I answered.

"Bye, Daisy." Evan looked as though he was grappling with how to make an exit.

Daisy wrapped her arms around her father's waist and smiled up at him.

"Bye, Daddy. I'll see you tomorrow."

For the rest of the night, "My dad says" and "When I get to Pennsylvania" dominated Daisy's conversation. It was good to hear her sound so enthusiastic, but I couldn't believe it would be so easy. She went to bed easily enough, but she was up and down all night with the series of small catastrophes six-year-old children are prone to after a day of too much excitement and vast quantities of the few kinds of junk food Daisy would willingly consume. I was summoned for dry bedding and to banish the monsters from the hall closet. On my second trip to supply a drink, I finally gave up and lay down with her.

"Are you feeling nervous, Daisy?"

"A little. I think I will miss my mommy. But my dad says I can call whenever I want to."

"Would you like me to tell you a story? How about 'The Three Bears'?"

"Could you tell about the little kids who get lost in the forest and eat the house?"

Daisy lay quietly in my arms. I told her the story of the ginger-bread house and the children who saved themselves and returned home to the parents who never stopped loving them.

The next morning I met Daisy's stepmother. Helen was as warm and quiet and unassuming as Evan. Their children, a boy of three and a girl of four, were sweet. They seemed so healthy. Sometimes I forget what normal looks like.

During the week that followed, Daisy spent much of her time with her family. She didn't return to school except for one afternoon to say good-bye. I felt a little cheated; this was my last week with Daisy. But if I found it a strain on me, I could only imagine how it must have felt to Daisy, torn and confused as she must have been by this sudden change in her life. She reacted with her usual array of anxious spinning and flapping. Still, there was a connection between Daisy and Evan that was unmistakable. He was able to calm her down with a hold similar to the one I used when she was out of control. It wasn't punishment or even really restraint. More like a reminder. "If you can't pull yourself together, I will help you until you are able."

All week I had been thinking about what to say to Daisy. We had talked, of course, but it felt like so much was still unsaid. I wasn't sure she even realized that I didn't want her to go. Bruce and I had been so busy trying to act excited about the move that we hadn't acknowledged our grief to her. I thought it was important to do that. Daisy needed to know she mattered to us.

I chose a Wednesday afternoon. The house was unnaturally quiet. The older children were all in school and the younger ones asleep. Daisy found me in the den looking through an old photo album. I pulled her onto my lap and held her close.

"Do you remember when you first came to us, Daisy? Look. I found this picture. We took it the day after you came. Do you remember Crystal and Priscilla and Jazzy?"

"Kind of. I think I was very scared. I remember I wetted my pants sometimes and I didn't eat."

"You've grown up a lot since then. You never wet your pants anymore, and now you eat lots of things."

Daisy looked worried. "I don't like beans. They won't make me eat beans, will they? I afraid of beans."

Daisy rocked in my lap. It was easy sometimes to forget how fragile she still was.

"They won't make you eat beans, honey. I told your dad that beans make you sick. He seems like a nice man, Daisy. I think he'll be a good dad."

"I think I sort of don't want to go, Kathy. It makes my tummy hurt when I think about it."

"You know what? It makes my tummy hurt, too. I'm so happy that you found your dad and that he can take good care of you, but I'm sad, too. I'm going to miss you, Daisy. You're a special little girl, and I love you very, very much. If you ever feel alone or scared, you can remember that. That I'm here, in this house, loving you."

"What if I don't want to go? Do I still have to?"

"You do, Daisy. I'm as sorry as I can be that you don't have more time to get used to the idea, but this is how it has to be."

Daisy sat for a minute without talking, her face buried in my shirt. When she looked up, I could see that she had been crying.

"Sometimes," she said, so quietly I had to strain to hear her. "Sometimes I wish you was my mom and I never had to move. I just want this to be home."

"Sometimes I wish that, too, Daisy. But that's the selfish part of me. The part that wants to keep you for myself because you're such a special little girl. The other part of me cares too much about you to keep you from your dad. He's your family, Daisy. The real deal. What's most important is that he loves you. All these years he never stopped thinking about and worrying about you. He's kept your picture in his wallet all this time. He came as soon as he knew you needed him."

"Will you keep my picture in your wallet, too?"

It took a moment before I was able to answer without my voice shaking. "I surely will, Daisy. And I would always come if you needed me."

At last the week was over. The bags were packed. There was a last-minute scramble. "Did you remember your toothbrush? Where is your library book? I need to return that. Is the red sweater yours?" It was the kind of talk designed to keep us from having too much time in which to say good-bye.

Lauren came to see Daisy off. I was glad she was there. She was a buffer between Daisy's new family and her old one. Her chatter filled up the awkward minutes it took to put Daisy's bags in the trunk and say good-bye. I don't remember what I said to Daisy in that last moment, probably because it was surely nothing profound. "Be good, sweetie. Make sure you send me pictures." They were the same empty words I used whenever children left. I didn't watch the car pull out of the driveway.

Bruce stayed home long enough to make sure I was all right. Lauren remained for a few minutes longer. We talked about our respective teenagers and the latest bestseller, everything but Daisy. I was relieved when she left and I could get to work.

I bathed Lakita and put her in a fresh outfit. I found the doll Lupe liked to play with while I cared for the baby and settled her down with the doll clothes. It was bottle time, nap time, play time. I was grateful for the immediacy of the children's needs. They left little time for much else. When they were both quiet, I pulled out everything from the kitchen junk drawer. I sorted and tossed and vowed to never let it become so out of control again. Then there was lunch to fix and the baby needed another bottle.

When it was quiet, I made a fresh pot of tea from my special stash a friend had brought me from England. I drank it from an antique china cup I keep on the top of the hutch. Then I pulled out my Godiva chocolates and ate two pieces. I ate them slowly and decided to call that lunch.

Tomorrow, I promised myself, I will clean Daisy's room. I will turn the mattress and put fresh sheets on the bed. Then I will call Susan and let her know we have an empty bed.

Twelve

❧

Daisy had been gone for two full months. Summer had reached the hill towns in Massachusetts, a full three weeks after it found the low-lying valleys. I felt as if I had finally come up for air. Hours could go by when I didn't think about Daisy, although I still found myself calling her in to dinner from time to time.

I had not heard from her. I had written to her twice, once a note enclosed in a box of letters that her former classmates had sent, then another brief note in a birthday card. I hadn't gotten a response after either. I had just stopped thinking that I would hear from her when I received a packet of pictures from Evan. They were wonderful pictures, my favorite kind. There were no posed, smile-for-the-camera photos in uncomfortable fancy clothes that no child in her right mind would ever really wear. These were all candid family shots: Daisy at the lake, Daisy looking at a book with her little sister, and Daisy with her head resting on the family dog. In my favorite picture, Daisy was holding one of Evan's hands in both of hers. She is wearing a typical Daisy outfit of wild mismatched colors and an outrageous flowered hat and laughing up into Evan's face. He is smiling down at her, as though he had just won the lottery—which in many ways he had. A short note said that they were all doing well, that Daisy liked her new therapist and seemed to be settling in. Evan also said that Glenna called often and planned to spend two weeks in Pennsylvania during the summer. There was no message to us from Daisy.

Although I was short on time that morning, I dug around in the back of my closet and pulled out the plastic bin that held the family pictures waiting to go into albums. They usually had a long wait. I envied my friends who seemed always to have their pictures in order, either by date or person or event. Mine were a mixed-up jumble, the only order being the layers. The farther down you dug in the box, the younger my children were. I didn't label anything, so should any of the kids bring the box out on a Sunday afternoon hoping to create some kind of order, we spent most of our time guessing and second-guessing one another as to who the extra children were.

"Is that Ashley?" one might ask.

"No, that's Michelle. She's the one who threw up on Grandma's suit. Ashley was the one who bit Daddy on the toe."

"Oh, my gosh! I didn't know we had this picture of me hold-ing Justin. He went home to his mother, didn't he?"

"Yep, but he came back into care last year. He's at the Law-sons' now. I think they plan to adopt."

Alone, with none of the family talk to distract me, I was able to sort through the pictures fairly quickly until I came to a bunch from the year Karen turned five. There were the beautiful princesses—Karen, Maggie, and Daisy—posing in their thrift-store finery. I found a sweet picture of Maggie handing Ben a drooping bouquet of dandelions, and one of Bruce rocking a small bundle I assumed was Lakita. I didn't start to cry until I found a picture of Karen and Daisy. They had fallen asleep to-gether on the sofa one rainy afternoon the week before Daisy left. Daisy's head was on the arm of the sofa. Karen was snug-gled next to her, her head almost in Daisy's lap. They looked nothing alike really, but there was a sense of connectedness be-tween them that is usually reserved for sisters.

I pulled myself together in time to put on a pot of coffee. A woman from our local paper was coming by to talk to me about what it was like to be a foster parent. She was doing a piece about our child welfare system. A small child had been killed by his foster mother a month earlier. The paper was full of stories about what needed to change if we were going to provide chil-dren with safe havens.

"So, tell me about it," she said, as we settled down over cof-fee and muffins. "What is it like to try to raise kids who belong to someone else and have such awful histories? You get paid about seventeen dollars a day. Is that right? So it's hard to believe that you do this just for the money. I mean, you could do better flipping hamburgers."

I thought for a minute before I answered. "Most of the time, what I do is just the work of any mother. It can be mind-numbingly boring. It's dishes and laundry and dentists and school lunches. Some days I feel as if my most significant accomplishment is sorting all the socks. Sometimes I think that if I hear one more chorus of "Baby Beluga," I will go smack out of my mind. Lots of days I care much more about whether the baby poops than I do about the state of the Union. On those days I have to wonder what on earth I have gotten myself into. This is a crazy life. I have a kid who can't go to school because she's moved twelve times and nobody can find her immunizations. I have kids who have their court cases continued five or six times because the adults can't organize themselves. I wonder if they have any idea how long the wait is when you're six and you just want to go home. There are grim days when the things my kids tell me are so sad and so awful I can digest only small pieces at a time. On those days, flipping hamburgers doesn't seem like such a bad idea."

"So why do you do it?" she asked.

Daisy's pictures were lying in a pile on the table between us. I fingered the one on top, the one of Daisy and Evan. It was just what I had been asking myself for weeks now.

"Sometimes there are really good days. Sometimes a mother will show up for a visit, and I can feel the love between her and this kid. She's clean and sober, and she's finished her parenting course. She's getting her daughter back, and I feel like I had a small part in this wonderful thing. Once, I remember, I got this little guy on one of those overnight hotline placements that lasted for the better part of two weeks. He was such a tough little bruiser but he really liked the babying he got from me. He loved getting tucked in with a story at night and having nice clothes and regular meals. He moved on to a regular placement but I ran into him with his new foster father about a month later at the mental health clinic. He saw me and his pudgy little face just lit up. 'Hey, lady,' he yelled, 'I remember you. You was nice at me.' This fostering life. It isn't usually about the big hurrahs. It's about moments for kids when they can remember clean sheets and hot chocolate and that somebody was nice at them."

After the interview ended and the reporter left, I realized it was time to do something I had been putting off. I had packed for Daisy. I had transferred her records and sent her on her way. But I had not really said good-bye. I took out my journal and wrote a letter I knew I would never send.

> *Dear Daisy,*
> *The sun is shining today. I am thinking of you with your family. I can see your smile and I know the sun is shining on you, too.*
> *All my love,*
> *Kathy*